The Meta Pattern

The Ultimate Structure of Influence for Coaches, Hypnosis Practitioners and Business Executives

By

Sarah Carson

and

Shawn Carson

Changing Mind Publishing

New York, NY

The Meta Pattern: The Ultimate Structure of Influence for coaches, hypnosis practitioners and business executives

NLP Mastery Series

Cover Design by Richie Williamson

Photography courtesy of Caroline Bergonzi

Editing by John Harten

Table of Contents

Acknowledgements

We are deeply indebted to John Overdurf for being the mastermind, creator and teacher of the Meta Pattern. Knowing and understanding this pattern has transformed how we do change work and has ultimately helped us to help so many clients let go of their problems and become more of who they already are.

We would like to acknowledge and recognize the fundamental work of Dr. Richard Bandler and John Grinder.

And to Jess Marion, our wonderful friend and business partner, our deep thanks for everything you do.

About the NLP Mastery Series

Within the NLP Mastery series, we analyze and explain NLP and HNLP patterns, techniques and principles. This series is focused towards furthering your knowledge of NLP and HNLP and deepening your understanding of change work and influence.

Each power-packed book builds into a full library that will make up an entire HNLP practitioner course and you can pick and chose whichever topic interests you, or start from the beginning and work your way through book by book. Either way is better, and I hope that whichever way you decide to use these books, you will enjoy learning something new, expand upon what you already know you know, and have a fun time doing so.

Foreword

By John Overdurf

It is my great pleasure to introduce this invaluable work by Sarah and Shawn Carson. They are true "students of the game" with a rich blend of curiosity, rigor, experience, high levels of competence, humor and the wisdom to not take themselves too seriously. Great attributes of people who can serve as your teachers in this book, don't you think?

So you can *begin to look forward to some deep learning*... and a perhaps a generous sprinkling of *"aha's"*...perhaps even a dash of OMG insightful edutainment... from their thorough exploration into one of the most powerful and simple patterns of change which has incredible scope of application. *Interested?*

So I'll start with a question which I often ask at coaching and therapy trainings I do: *"What is the pattern which underlies all classic and well-formed NLP change work,* any effective psychotherapeutic and hypnotherapy technique, shamanic processes as well as sales, consulting, public speaking - and perhaps many other areas of which I am ignorant but *you could be curious about discovering, yourself?"* It is the structure of purposeful change.

In fact, it is a template for which you can create myriad conversational change patterns on the fly. Why? Because it only has four steps or phases you have to remember. It is a roadmap that will help you know where you are in a change process and what needs to be done to create the desired change. It's also effective for troubleshooting when something isn't working, why it isn't, and what can be done to right the course.

Curious? Or perhaps you already know, because the secret's been out for quite a while! It's something I like to call the Meta Pattern, i.e., the Mother of all NLP patterns, and as far as I can tell, a pretty decent modeling of any type of effective change regardless of the context in which you're looking.

My intent in this foreword is to give you my take with a few things I've learned along the way, not to provide you with all the details or applications as Sarah and Shawn have done an outstanding job in doing all that for you…and more!

So if there's some points during the following section where you think, "Hmm, but how do you do that?" or "Why this way?" or other questions it means your brain is functioning really well. Your brain is priming itself to sort for what's important to you so *you will learn* more *easily* and *deeply*.

OK, so I must be honest and tell you many folks have asked me over the years why I didn't write a book about the Meta Pattern - or even this one. The answer is not a simple one, but I can tell you this: some times it works a lot better when someone else delivers your baby rather than doing it yourself. Ask any mother this and she'll most likely agree! That said, I'm still raising a baby who's now a precocious teenager, so there are many more developments you can look forward to in the future!

So, what is the Meta Pattern is why is it useful?

Think of the Meta Pattern as a way to chunk and sequence purposeful change.

Let's say you have a "problem": you are given a lot of raw data you really need to remember, and you need to remember it easily and quickly. Additionally, you are going to have to remember a lot of other information simultaneously! So if you spend all your 7 plus or minus 2 chunks of attention on that, there will be no other working memory space to pay attention to other things.

For example, how about something like the sequence of numbers below. You only have a few seconds to memorize it and then remember it completely. So turn this page after five seconds and see if you can remember it, then come back to this page.
Ready…go

64, 4, 144, 25, 49, 9, 121, 16, 1, 81, 100, 36

Welcome back. *Now… take a nice, deep breath…*
and consider:

How can you create a model, which will make this data easy to remember, use and teach to others?

Well, lets's see, you could put them in some sort of sequence. perhaps smallest to largest, or vice-versa. So let's start with: 1, 4, 9, 16, 25, 36, 49, 64, 81, 100, 121, 144.

You could memorize this data in a sequence and that would make it a little easier, right? But remember, you need to know it almost instantly so you can pay attention to other things!

This is where looking deeper for a pattern becomes a critical step. Hmm… Is there an underlying pattern of the above sequences?

There is. You know what it is? They are all square roots.

$1^2, 2^2, 3^2, 4^2, 5^2, 6^2, 7^2, 8^2, 9^2, 10^2, 11^2, 12^2$

Now back to the original problem— "...you are given a lot of raw data you need to remember, and you need to remember it easily and quickly."
Think you can do it now? You bet you can. That is why the Meta Pattern is useful:
you can remember it easily and quickly. It is an easy way to chunk and sequence change. By the way, this was also an example of the process in action!

So here's the Meta Pattern - replete with classic NLP terminology:

Associate to the "Problem" or Present state

Dissociate from the "problem" or Present State

Associate to Resource State(s)

Associate Resource States to "Problem" or "Present" State.

Let me give you just a few highlights for using this pattern in the context of coaching and therapy, for ease of explanation, but I can tell you I use this process in consulting, teaching and presenting in many other contexts. I'll leave those details for Sarah and Shawn.

1. Associate to the Problem or Present State (PS)

This is is the phase where the neural networks of the "presenting issue" or "problem state" (PS) is elicited in sensory-based language. As I like to say, this where you are "stalking the wild synesthesia," which is what you get paid the big bucks to do. You are wanting to find the precise trigger for the issue; what causes the automatic reaction of an unwanted response. There is a lot to this in terms of technique, so I won't go into all that here, but you can find some more on this later in the book. For now, though, here are some reasons why you want to get really good at lighting-up the neural networks of the PS:

The first reason is based on neuroplasticity research. This is the brain's ability to physically change itself in response to what is happening in the context and/or where attention is directed. The only time a circuit is actually plastic is when it is lit up. If we do not light up the circuit it will not change when the resource is applied.

Secondly, there's the research on re-consolidation of *memory*. This research finding is without a doubt one of the most important discoveries in the history of psychotherapy.
This is the molecular unlocking and re-locking of the synapses of an altered memory or representation. When a sensory based, associated memory/representation is brought into consciousness it becomes as labile, malleable, plastic as it was when it was first encoded. Whatever is introduced during this re-consolidation window will write over the original representation.

In other words, what is occurring in the context at the time will update the pre-existing representation; it can even delete it. In less than 6 hours, this automatic, molecular process re-locks the new synaptic connections creating a new locked memory. Similar to the encoding of an original representation, which can takes weeks, the new re-consolidated representation takes more time to fully complete the structural processes of the re-wired synapses.

This amazing process will not happen if the PS is not elicited in sensory based language! Very important!

Third is something practical. We need to have the exact trigger of the PS that we can say in a few words, voice tone and/ or a gesture, a look, so we have handle or anchor of the PS to activate it at will. This becomes critical when we get to the final step when we connect the Resource state(s) to the PS. We need something simple, so the process happens quickly without conscious mediation. But more about that later.

2. Dissociate from the PS

Now that the above conditions have been met, we need to get the client out of that state for an outcome, resource or end state to be elicited. If we do not do this, the client will be in the state-bound thinking and experience of the world which is inside of the problem. If they would continue to be associated to the PS and you ask them for example, "How do you want to be different?" the likely response will be something like "I don't want to be (the problem.)" Essentially they will be demonstrating all the things they think, say, feel, and do when they are in the problem. Why? Because memories/internal representations are state-bound.

So it's important that you change your voice tone and tempo and physiology sufficiently enough it prompts a change in the client's physiology, so s/he can access some new thinking and access more resourceful state.

In my experience, the most crucial steps in the pattern are these first two. If you have a handle on the PS and know how to light it up so it's plastic and then you've gotten the client out of the PS, you've already started laying the tracks for success change.

3. Associate to Resource State(s) (RS)

This is where you assist the client in accessing states which facilitate the desired outcome. There are many nuances to this and frankly thousands of ways to do this which involve different combinations and sequences of linguistic patterns accompanied by non-verbal analogues to coax out a big robust resource state that will eventually collapse the problem.

All these linguistic and non-verbal patterns are often are what fascinate those who are new to this kind of work. They can be basic or very flashy. You can use non-linear inductive language patterns (which actually can accomplish the second step and this one) or just straight forward questions like "How do you want to feel or be instead?" and then continue questioning until the state lights up. You can "catch" someone in a spontaneous state, perhaps not even one you planned. You might have even misspoke, but if it generates a resource state, anchor it and use it!

Yet, at the end of the day, any of these are only as good as the set-up: making sure you've previously lit up the neural networks related to the problem.

The key criterion to keep in mind here is the RS needs to be more robust than the PS. You are looking for wide-spread neural activation, which means you see some *big shifts* in the physiology that do not look like the physiology of the PS. In most cases, they will look like the opposite of the PS. There are exceptions, so if you're interested, you can learn about those in later sections of the book. You will also hear a concomitant change in voice tone, tempo, pitch, and locus when the client accesses the resource state.

At this point in the process, you need to have a handle or anchor through the use of a word, voice tone and/or physiological analogue to that you can elicit the state quickly. Basically, it needs to meet the same conditions as the anchor for the PS: something short and sweet, as you want to be able to elicit the state faster than the client can think. In that way, you are engaging the *change at the unconscious level*, below the level of conscious processing which in the end will make it as resilient as the problem was.

4. Associate Resource State(s) to Problem State. (Connect RS to PS)

This is where the two neural networks are connected. In classic NLP this is known as "the collapse;" You are literally re-wiring the brain at this point. For expediency, I usually get the person in the RS and then quickly take them to the trigger of the PS. I'll repeat this until the PS physiology and/or voice tone is no longer present. Since they are already in the RS it is much easier to just take them over to the trigger. No break state is necessary or even desirable a this point.

You want to know what will make your work easier and more successful at this point? Realize this is not a once a done maneuver. It's all about multiple iterations and recursion, because that is actually how the nervous system learns things in the first place, so we are applying the same principle here.

So, once you know you have a robust RS you take the person to the trigger, then observe and ask. "What's happening, now?" If the PS collapses and the person stays more in the RS, then whatever they say will be additional words, gestures and other analogues that you use in the next iteration. These will all be neural networks which are in some way connected to the RS. As you continue this process, it's kind of like starting with a small snow ball of resources at the top of the hill and you are rolling it down the hill, collecting more and more, as it gets bigger. This adds neurological complexity to the resource which will make it more resilient.

At the time you connect the two, speed is of the essence when you connect the PS and RS. That's why you need to have simple handles for each of the states. Alternatively, if you use some sort of ambiguity or non-linear linguistic construction at

14

the time of the collapse, it will temporarily suspend conscious/dominant hemispheric functioning and will accomplish the same effect as speed. It will re-wire the brain below the level of conscious awareness.

One other little important piece: Remember at the beginning of the section I said it's easier when the client is in the RS to take them to the PS? It is, but, it is not the sequence which naturally occurs in the real world! It is just a easy way to "glue" them together to get things rolling.

Eventually you need to run the sequence in the natural sequence which occurs in the real world. In other words the trigger needs to come first. You fire the trigger of the PS then the anchors for the RS. You actually want what was the trigger of the PS to now be the trigger of the RS. Do this until it's as automatic as the problem was. Straight classical conditioning! At this point, you have re-wired the brain below the level of conscious mediation so it will be as resilient as the problem was. And, there you have it the pattern from beginning to end with a few nuances to hopefully get you thinking.

Just one more thing…In closing, for me, the highest level of the intent of teaching is to enable others to take what you have developed and taught and really run with it. How can a falcon soar when it's "owner" won't release it from it's tethers? It is with this Spirit I whole heartedly support Sarah and Shawn's sincerity and effort in getting this information out to those who can use it ethically and beneficially with others. They are near and dear to me as friends and colleagues and they are stars on the rise. Enjoy their light!

OK, that's it, enough with all this….. Hopefully this little amuse-bouche has whetted your appetite for the coming appetizers and the main course. The chefs are ready when *you are ready…* and you know what it's like when *your mouth is beginning to water……*when you are *looking forward* to something really tasty… come on…*that's right….*that's because your *unconscious* is hungry…… for *learning.* *Fill up on the goodness while you read on!*

John Overdurf
Phoenix October 8, 2014

Introduction

Welcome to the Meta Pattern, the structure of persuasive communication. This model was first developed by world-renowned coach, HNLP (Humanistic Neuro Linguistic Psychology) trainer and corporate consultant John Overdurf, to describe the process that all effective coaches, speakers, and business people lead their clients through in order to change emotions and behaviors. The Meta Pattern is a simple sequence of four steps that underlies each and every NLP pattern ever created, all effective coaching and hypnosis techniques, and the most influential advertisements and sales processes. Once you fully and completely understand the Meta Pattern, you will be able to quickly and easily grasp any new pattern you may come across, as well as gain mastery over those you already know. Sound like a big claim? Read on.

Not only does the Meta Pattern underlie all of NLP, it underlies any piece of coaching or (non pharmaceutical drug-related) therapeutic change work. Sound like a big claim? Read on.

This structure also appears in all influence modalities including teaching, management, sales and marketing, and politics. If you want to understand what is going on around you, learn and begin to apply the Meta Pattern to your life.

Before we get to the actual steps of the Meta Pattern, we will describe our own experiences in learning it. Learning the Meta

Pattern is a process. At first the pattern will appear almost childishly simple, so simple that you will not believe it can explain everything. Next you will begin to apply the Meta Pattern by trying to force the steps of an NLP pattern within it, and you'll find that they don't fit. Finally, as you begin to master the Meta Pattern, you will realize that it provides a much deeper and more profound understanding of the patterns that we use. This is what NLP Mastery is all about.

Shawn's Story

I was first introduced to the Meta Pattern in the summer of 2007. I was already a Master Practitioner of NLP and a certified hypnotist, but looking back, I am not sure how I was able to do any coaching or change work without understanding the fundamental principles of change embodied within the Meta Pattern. I had gone to attend my NLP trainers' training in Scottsdale with the amazing NLP Master Trainers John Overdurf and Julie Silverthorne. John was teaching an 'optional' evening program on conversational coaching. I say 'optional' because the students hung on every word John had to say and we would not have considered missing anything, optional or not.

John was teaching his Coaching Pattern and was explaining the Meta Pattern, the pattern underlying all change work, and all NLP patterns in particular. As he explained the steps of the pattern, my analytical mind began to go into overdrive. I began to analyze all NLP patterns I knew to see whether this was indeed the Holy Grail of NLP I had been seeking. For some patterns, such as the Circle of Excellence, which we will consider shortly, the fit was obvious, but for others, the Meta Pattern was much harder to spot.

I thought about the Swish pattern. In the Swish, at least as classically taught, your resourceful self is seen in a dissociated way, as if looking at a lifelike picture of your ideal self. How

18

does this fit with the first step of the Meta Pattern, which demands that we associate into the resource?

I thought about the Visual Squash, in which two competing parts are visualized on the palms of the hands, while a virtual negotiation takes place. How does this fit in with the second step of the Meta Pattern, which demands that we dissociate from the problem?

Later on in the book we will reveal the secret of how the Meta Pattern underlies such diverse NLP Patterns as the Swish, the Visual Squash, the V-K Dissociation, the Six-Step Reframe, and others. Once you understand the power of the Meta Pattern in explaining each and every NLP pattern, you will be a true master of NLP, but for now we will leave the secret veiled in mystery!

(Any readers interested in discovering the true power of the Swish or Visual Squash can read our book *The Swish* and our book *The Visual Squash*, both by Shawn Carson and Jess Marion.)

I realized that unlocking the mystery of the Meta Pattern was going to take me some time, so I turned my attention back to the matter in hand, focusing on John's Coaching Pattern. Returning to New York, I discussed the Meta Pattern with the trainers I took Practitioner and Master Practitioner with. They were unaware of the pattern, and to my eager mind, strangely incurious about it. After all, if there is a simple four-step pattern which underlies all NLP patterns, then I would never need to be concerned about getting the steps right, or whether I had forgotten a step, or done the steps in the right order. I could simply trust the Meta Pattern to guide me.

Sarah's Story

When I was first learning NLP, I was so excited to uncover what had been going on in my own 'world' within myself and in others. I went to class each Friday eager and excited to learn something new about the world around me and to discover more about myself.

As the wonderful world of NLP began to open up, we moved into learning the classic, standard patterns of NLP: the Swish, the Six Step Reframe, the Fast Phobia Fix, Stuck Meta Resource, the Visual Squash and more (maybe some of these are familiar to you, or perhaps I have whetted your appetite to learn more!).

Although still fascinated by the study, I felt there had been a shift. It seemed that my study had become less holistic and had become more about learning and remembering the steps of a pattern, about getting them in the right order and just moving my partner through each step without really having any idea of the purpose behind each step. Each week, a new pattern was taught, adding to my catalogue of knowledge and to my NLP toolkit, but I still felt that I lacked the guidance of a common structure. I needed something to pin them all on. By the end of my NLP Practitioner, I had learned around 20 patterns but had an increasing feeling of overwhelm; which pattern do I use and when? What do I do if the pattern 'doesn't work'? The standard answer of 'do something different' just seemed to be a brush off, and I craved something more.

About 4 months after having completed my NLP Practitioner, I learned about John Overdurf and Julie Silverthorn and their HNLP model. HNLP is Humanistic Neuro Linguistic Psychology, and as soon as I heard the name it just felt right, somehow more complete, and I was soon enrolled on a Master Practitioner Course with John down in Atlanta.

Early on the first day of class, John began to explain the Meta Pattern that he taught in his Practitioner class. There were a few folks in the class like me who had taken our NLP Practitioner class elsewhere and John was keen for us all to be on the same page. As John began to outline this pattern, it was as though the clouds parted and the light began to shine through. This was it! This was the building block I had been searching for, the fundamental structure that underpinned all the patterns I had learned. Not only that, it was just 4 straightforward steps, super simple to remember and easy to recall. It made complete and utter sense; I now had a simple, uncomplicated framework through which to move my clients, and it gave me the knowledge of exactly where I was in each step, in what direction to take the next step, and how to take it.

That evening I sat in my hotel room and studied all of the NLP patterns I had been taught, and fitted them into the structure of the Meta Pattern. I found that they all elegantly fit the pattern, that it provided me with the simple, yet powerful methodology for change and that I had just discovered the missing element that would allow me to fully understand the process of change and to help make me a really effective change worker.

About this book

Within this book we will be looking at the HNLP's Meta Pattern. You will learn the 4 steps of the Meta Pattern and along the way begin to understand why NLP Patterns contain certain steps in a certain order, to utilize the client's own neurology for change.

We will then share how applicable this pattern is by exploring how it is used as the structure for change in all NLP Patterns, in coaching, in hypnosis, and also for self-coaching.

After exploring the Meta Pattern in the context of change work and coaching, we will widen our frame to the world of influence. Will give you a glimpse of how great politicians and speechwriters, leaders and managers, salesman and storytellers all use the Meta Pattern to influence their audience, whether they know it or not.

Before we begin, let me ask you this:

Have you ever worked with a coaching client, and found the pattern or technique you were using did not go as well as you would have liked?
Do you get caught up in getting the steps of an NLP pattern 'right'?
Would you like to have a surefire way of knowing exactly where you are at any given time, in any given change process?
Would you like to know where you are leading your client, and why you are leading them there, during their change?
Would you like to be certain that you are effecting change on a neurological level and know exactly how to do that?
Would you like to be more influential, increasing your sales, more effectively leading your team, or able to give a speech on the spur of the moment?

Then the Meta Pattern of HNLP is exactly what you need. It provides you with a straightforward, powerful and elegant framework in just 4 easy steps. By knowing and understanding these steps, you will always know exactly where you are in any piece of change work.

The elegance of this pattern comes from the fact that within its simplicity is the direct utilization of your client's neurology. In order to effect real change with a client, we have to be able to activate the neurological networks associated with the problem and their desired outcome. We will expand upon this is more detail later in the book, and suffice it to say that when you know you are doing this, you know precisely *how* to do this and you know exactly *why* you are doing this, then you will see dramatic results with your clients…and this is ultimately what we all want!

The Meta Pattern utilizes a familiar unconscious pattern. The 4 steps of the Meta Pattern follow the structure of advertising commercials, powerful political speeches, effective sales copy, movies, stories and so much more. This is a pattern that is known and recognized on a deep unconscious level probably by everybody on the planet. By understanding the Meta Pattern, you are tapping into the Collective Unconscious.

I have never had a client tell me that they have consciously "decided to do" their problem. No one says, "Well I just woke up one day and thought…'you know I'm going to bite my nails…that seems like a good idea.' No, each client comes in and says something like, "I don't know why/how I do this, my fingers just seem to be in my mouth before I know it!" Or, "I do it because of something that happened to me in childhood." This is because the problem is in the unconscious mind; it has come to the client's conscious awareness and they have tried conscious ways to overcome it. A conscious solution to an unconscious problem is doomed to fail.

We need to access the unconscious mind in order to figure out how the client is doing their problem, to access appropriate resources, and place these resources in exactly the right place to effect change. This sounds like a daunting task, but using the Meta Pattern as the guiding structure allows us to lead the client through an unconsciously familiar process, towards the outcome they desire. Our understanding of this process gives us, the change worker, a precise roadmap of where the client is at any point during a session, where they come from, and where they are going.

The Meta Pattern also gives you the opportunity to objectively review your work and understand where it may have faltered, and highlight the places where your work can be improved. As change workers, we are always looking for ways to enhance our skills, and by taking the time to review and take another look at our practice will serve to make us even better and more effective in our work. So we encourage you to begin to review your work on a regular basis. Learn and grow from your mistakes and remember there is 'no failure, only feedback.'

Chapter One:

The History of the Meta Pattern

In our first NLP Mastery book, *The Swish*, we included our take on the history of the pattern. A number of people gave us feedback that they were really not interested in the history of the pattern; they just wanted us to dive into the pattern itself, and how they could use it.

Therefore, in our second NLP Mastery book, *The Visual Squash*, we omitted any discussion of the history of the pattern. We then had several people tell us how much they had enjoyed the history chapter in *The Swish*, and how disappointed they were we had not included a similar chapter in *The Visual Squash*.

So this book we are compromising. We are including a chapter on the history of the Meta Pattern, as we understand it, but we give you full permission not to read this chapter if you would prefer to simply dive right in to the pattern itself. We promise you there is nothing within this chapter that is 'required reading' for you to understand the chapters that follow.

The Meta Pattern has been around since the dawn of civilization. It provides the basis for the Hindu spiritual text the *Bhagavad Gita*, as well as Homer's *Odyssey*. Even Jesus Christ uses it to underpin his Sermon on the Mount.

Of course, going back this far forces us to find the common link between these classics of Eastern and Western religions and cultures, so let's start our study in more recent history!

The Meta Pattern was developed (or discovered) by John Overdurf.
John got on to the Meta Pattern and began teaching it when he was teaching the linguistic module for Tad James' Master Practitioner Trainings in Hawaii in the early nineties. John has a knack for extracting the most important principles from NLP and coaching, and for him, this was the pattern underlying all the classic NLP change work patterns, and was most obviously displayed in a simple collapsing anchors maneuver. He called it "The Meta Pattern, a.k.a. The Mother of All NLP Patterns."

Later, when in preparation for a Master Practitioner Training in Lancaster, PA in the mid nineties, his co-trainer and wife at the time, Julie Silverthorn, wanted to model how John did language patterns. They spent a number of evenings where she'd present an issue and then John would attempt to work the issue through conversationally, then they would discuss the structure and sequencing. All of this was later codified into their Beyond Words Model which featured the Meta Pattern as the chief way to structure linguistic interventions on the fly (more on this below).

The Meta Pattern appears ridiculously simple, too simple for its own good. Something this simple surely can't be powerful. And yet it is; in many ways, the Meta Pattern forms the basis of HNLP.

As John began to extensively explore phone coaching it became more difficult to do traditional NLP patterns using kinesthetic or spatial anchors, formal trance processes, and so on. As a result, John had to redesign HNLP to include purely conversational versions of each of the NLP patterns. The only thing that made this possible was his deep understanding of the purpose of each step of each pattern, based upon the Meta Pattern itself. Not only did the Meta Pattern allow John to create conversational versions of each pattern, but also new patterns began to emerge almost spontaneously from the Meta Pattern. Probably the most important and fundamental of these is John's Coaching Pattern. Sometimes, when I'm (Shawn) teaching the Swish, I describe the Coaching Pattern as the conversational version of the Swish, however you could equally consider it to be conversational version of Stuck-Meta-Resource, or indeed any number of other classical NLP patterns depending on where the emphasis is placed in the Coaching Pattern.

It is equally true that the HNLP Coaching Pattern is unique pattern in and of itself, with significant differences from any existing NLP Pattern. The Coaching Pattern arises simply, and almost inevitably, from the Meta Pattern.

John's next step down this new pathway came by focusing on the second step of the Meta Pattern, dissociating from the Present State. Again, focusing on conversational change, John began to explore how he could dissociate a client from a problem when the problem had become so solidified in the client's mind that it colored the very way they thought. As result of focusing on this second step of the Meta Pattern, John developed his simple yet unique Beyond Words pattern. Combining the principles of Beyond Words with the Meta Pattern, John extended his linguistic alchemy to Attention Shifting Coaching, a complete conversational coaching model built around the Meta Pattern.

The 4 steps of the Meta Pattern

Before we get back to our story, we need to understand the four steps of the Meta Pattern. The first step is to get in touch with (we say 'associate into') one state of being, which we will call the Problem State or Present State. In the context of change work, this will be the state that the client wants to change.

The second and third steps are to leave that first state of being, and get in touch with, or associate into, a new state of being, which we will call the Resource States.

The final step of the Meta Pattern is to get in touch with both Problem State and Resource State at the same time.

To put it in the most straightforward terms:

1. Associate into the Problem or Present State

2. Dissociate from the Problem or Present State

3. Associate into the Resource State

4. Collapse the two states by bringing the Resource State to the Problem State

It is OK if this sounds confusing at the moment; rest assured we will go through each of the steps in detail in later chapters. We also explain the neuroscience behind the process in the next chapter.

At this stage, the key thing about this description is that there are two states of being which are fighting for control of the individual. These two states can be virtually anything, for example:

In the *Bhagavad Gita*, the first state is pain that the warrior Arjuna experiences as he is about it ride into battle against his family. His is lost in the illusion of a 'real' world. This is in contrast to the true nature of reality eventually revealed to him by the god Krishna.

28

In Homer's *Odyssey*, the two states for the hero, Odysseus, are represented first by the Trojan War and the siege of Troy, and second by his peaceful existence on Ithaca.

In Jesus' Sermon on the Mount, the first state is the *Old Testament's* teaching of "an eye for an eye." The second state is Jesus' completion of these teachings: "Turn the other cheek."

Two States of Being and Change Work

Before the rise of modern scientific investigation, it was believed by many cultures that mental and physical illness were the result of a battle between two entities for the right to possess a physical body. This fight was between the individual and an invading spirit who would attempt to gain entry in to the physical world.

Archaeologists and anthropologists report that some civilizations would drill holes in the skulls of the mentally ill in order to release the evil spirits which were seeking to possess them. The Catholic Church would use the ritual of exorcism for a similar purpose through the 18th century, and indeed to a more limited extent through the present day.

As change work became more scientifically based, various theories to explain mental illness gained and lost popularity. Some considered it to be genetic, passed down from parent to child. Others considered it to be organic, caused by some physical illness of the brain.

Finally, a student of Anton Mesmer, the Marquis de Puysegur, discovered that some of his patients displayed radically different personalities under hypnosis. This led to the work of Sigmund Freud, and more particularly Carl Jung curing mental illness by reintegrating these different personalities.

If we consider Jung and Freud's work from the frame of the Meta Pattern, this is exactly what they were doing. They were identifying two conflicting personalities or states, and seeking to reintegrate them by having the client experience, or become aware of, both at the same time.

This conflicting-state model perhaps came to its peak under Gregory Bateson's theory of double binds. This theory suggests that some psychological problems may arise from incongruous messages given to a child, perhaps by a parent or caregiver. These messages might well be given in different representational systems, for example a mother might get angry at her child, and shout, "How can you behave this way when I love you and do so much for you!" The mother's words state that she loves the child, but her tonality and physiology suggest otherwise, and the child is left to make sense of this contradiction.

In Fritz Perls' Gestalt Therapy, the two personalities or states identified might be imagined sitting in different chairs. The client will be asked to move from one chair to the other, at first experiencing each personality separately. Over the course of a session, or a number of sessions, the two personalities would be slowly reintegrated, perhaps by asking one to seek advice from the other.

This conflicting-states model was also very strongly embedded in the original version of NLP described in Richard Bandler and John Grinder's book *The Structure of Magic*. *The Structure of Magic* was written as a model of the therapeutic methods of Perls and Satir, rather than the particular NLP patterns developed later. It describes the use the NLP Meta Model (a model of language, not to be confused with the Meta Pattern!) to identify an 'incongruity.' This incongruity might be represented by a particular state (perhaps anger or fear) arising in a particular context, which did not seem justified by the context itself.

30

Let's take a quick example. You have a client who comes to see you because they are having problems at work. You explore the issue and find that whenever their boss appears, even if he is not speaking to them, they begin to feel uncomfortable, even afraid, and their work suffers. Of course their boss begins to notice and criticize them, making the problem worse. The original NLP model would suggest that there is a 'part' which is reacting inappropriately to the presence of their boss, and a part that would like to react more 'normally.' The practitioner might then separate those parts by placing each on a separate chair, and then ask the client to sit in each chair in turn to first explore, and then to reintegrate, these parts. Of course Gestalt techniques such as this were only some of many techniques Bandler and Grinder used.

Once again, viewed through this very simple lens, the Meta Pattern becomes blindingly obvious; there are two parts, one in each chair. The client is asked to sit in the first chair (associating into the first part), then step out of the first chair (dissociating from the first part) and sit in a second chair (associating into the second part), and then to slowly reintegrate (associating into both parts simultaneously).

So far so good. But then Bandler and Grinder moved the goal-posts. Rather than only describing how therapeutic change takes place by modeling outstanding therapists such as Milton Erickson, Virginia Satir and Fritz Perls, instead they decided to develop their own form of therapy called NLP. Within NLP there would be any number of specific change patterns that became known within the NLP world by such exotic names as the Swish, the Visual Squash, the 6-Step Reframe and so on. Taking an NLP practitioner course became an exercise in memorizing complex patterns, rather than understanding the structure of change work itself.

This process has come full circle in HNLP, with the development of the Meta Pattern: a return to the roots of NLP as a model for understanding change.

Chapter Two:

The Neuroscience of The Meta Pattern

When teaching a new pattern, we like to explain how that pattern affects the brain. After all, if there is no change in the structure of the brain as a result of experiencing a pattern, then there is no change in person. In this chapter we will consider several different principles from neuroscience that underlie the Meta Pattern and explain how the Meta Pattern uses these mechanisms to alter the wiring of the brain and effect change.

State Dependent Learning

State dependent learning is a principle of neuroscience that the learnings and memories that are accessible to you depend upon the state you are in at the time you wish to recall them, compared to the state you were in when you learned them. If you are in the same state, then you are more likely to be able to access the memories and learnings.

The state you are in may depend upon the environment you are in as well as other sensory information you are receiving, and also the emotions you are feeling. For example, research has been done on college students that indicates that they recall information better if they sit the test in the room in which they learned the same information. Even more surprising, they recall the information better if the same scent is sprayed both on the walls in which they learned the information and the room in which they are tested. The smell itself helps them to recall the relevant information. What this means in practice is that each and every piece of your experience calls to mind the other missing pieces of that same experience.

State dependent learning, in the context of change work, can be thought of as the neuroscience version of the 'rose-colored' spectacles; when you are in a positive state, everything in your world and everything in your experience appears to be positive. And similarly, when you're in a negative state, everything in your world and everything in your experience appears to be negative.

This explains why, when your client is in their problem, immersed in the negative state, and you ask them to think of an appropriate resource, they very often say they can't find one or that they just don't want the problem. For example, a client, Claudia, comes to you and says:

Client: I have a fear of flying.
Coach: How do you want to feel differently?
Client: I don't want to feel afraid.

The client tells you how they don't want to feel, not how they want to feel that's different.

Hebb's Law

Every thought, experience, event, concept or idea that we have has an effect in our brain. Whenever we think of something, we actually light up a specific set of neurons in our brain. The more frequently this event and its subsequent emotions are accessed, the stronger that network of neurons becomes. It is just like building up a muscle; it becomes easier and easier to 'light up' the connections and easier and easier to access the emotion. This process is known as Hebb's Law.

Hebb's Law is one of the few principles of neuroscience that is fairly universally agreed on and therefore can be called a 'law.' Hebb's Law itself is a complicated mathematical formula describing how neurons and neural networks become wired together in the brain, but is often stated as the principle that:

Neurons that fire together, wire together.

Hebb's Law helps to explain the principle of state dependent learning. When you are learning in a particular environment, say a classroom with a particular scent sprayed on the wall, then several networks are firing at the same time: the network representing the classroom, the network representing the sense, and the network representing the information to be learned. Because of Hebb's Law, these three circuits become wired together and essentially become one giant circuit. Later on, when you smell the same scent, the entire circuit lines up and you remember both the classroom and the information you learned there.

Hebb's Law and Problems

When someone has a problem, the tendency is to turn it over and over and over in the mind, each time strengthening the neural connections

So when a client comes to us with an issue or a problem that they have had for a long time or that they "always" feel, they have been doing a wonderful job of strengthening the neurological network aligned with their issue. Now, of course this is happening largely unconsciously; the client is unlikely to have been making themselves feel bad on purpose, and if they have, then that is a different issue entirely! Either way, however, the structure of the neurological network associated with their problem has become strong and more easily accessed than they would like.

These neurons have been firing together for a period of time and have now become synonymous with each other, have actually connected with each other and now are neurologically wired together.

Lets take an example of how this can happen:

Johnny is a little boy in kindergarten and one day it is his turn to do 'show and tell.' Although initially excited about showing his toy, he fumbles over his words; someone in class laughs at him and Johnny begins to feel anxious. He has just fired the "presentation" neurological network and the "anxious" network at the same time. (Obviously, the 'anxiety' feeling is also the result of the brain secreting hormones and chemicals which lead to the body reacting in negative way too...it is all linked!)

One small event like this is unlikely to cause performance anxiety, however, there is another time when Johnny has to read aloud in class and he gets the words wrong and feels anxious again. The same "performance/anxiety" network is lit up and begins to grow stronger. The neurons are beginning to link together and form a single entity. All too soon there is another event where Johnny has to perform and it leads to him even more quickly feeling anxiety as the neurons that are firing together are now wiring together. It is easy to see how performance anxiety can manifest when we observe its genesis from the point of view of Hebb's Law.

Now, the same can be said of positive states too. Janey may have a great time doing her first show and tell, easily reads aloud to the class and becomes a star performer because she has linked together "performance" with "confidence." In fact, whichever emotional state, positive or negative, experienced within a certain context becomes linked to that context. And the next time the person is in that context, the more likely they are to experience that state.

Long-Term Potentiation (LTP)

LTP refers to a neurological process where two neural networks that fire at the same time become more sensitive to each other. You can think of it as the forerunner of Hebb's Law, because this sensitivity ultimately becomes more permanent wiring.

As a coach, LTP allows you to literally begin rewiring your client's brain by associating them into a resourceful state, hence lighting up the networks associated with that state, and then asking them to think about the context in which they want the change to take place, lighting up that neural network. Initially the two neural networks, one for the resourceful state and one for the context of the change, become more sensitive to each other and more likely to fire off together.

Now, by using repetition, we can begin to make this wiring more permanent by first breaking their state (asking them to think of something else), and then re-triggering both the resourceful state and the context. Repeating this several times allows Hebb's Law to wire the two neural networks together so that they will automatically feel resourceful in that context.

Emotions as a Mind-Body Phenomena

Emotions, certainly primary emotions such as fear, anger, love and so on, can be thought of as mind-body states created by neuro transmitters, such as dopamine, which control the responses of various neurons in the brain, and other neuro-chemicals such as adrenaline, which control the reaction of the body, such as heart rate, breathing, and blood flow.

Therefore, emotional states can change as fast as, but only as fast as, another can replace one set of neuro transmitters and chemicals. As a rule of thumb, these chemical washes have a lifespan in the brain or body of around 90 seconds. Of course this is a generalization, and the actual length of the emotional states will depend upon their nature and intensity; for example, someone who has just successfully completed their first parachute jump is likely to experience an adrenaline rush for much longer than 90 seconds after they land!

Of course, many people experience states for much longer than 90 seconds. How does this happen? People are able to maintain states for relatively long periods of time by re-stimulating them, for example if you are watching your favorite sports team play an important match, you might well be in a state of heightened excitement for the whole of the game as you are watching it, as well as a period of time before and after when you were thinking about it. This stimulation of the state can be external (watching the game), or internal (thinking about the game). This is an example of how someone maintains a positive state for more than 90 seconds. Many people also use the same formula for maintaining negative states too.

In a coaching context, this 90-second rule can be very useful. It suggests that we can change the client's emotional state simply by waiting 90 seconds. Of course, to prevent them from re-triggering the state, we have to stop them from thinking about it by distracting them in some way. We will be talking about how we can do this in the chapter on dissociation.

Neural Darwinism

Neural Darwinism is a principle of neuroscience stating that neural networks that no longer fire are subject to pruning; links between the neurons in the network are literally severed until the network becomes incapable of firing. It is as though a new pathway in the forest has been forged and the old pathway becomes overgrown. The more the new pathway is used, the less the old one is until it becomes so overgrown that eventually all traces of what was have been entirely erased.

The Quantum Zeno Effect

When doing the Meta Pattern, we are continually shifting the client's attention around. We ask the client to focus on the context of the problem, and then away from the context of the problem to somewhere else, anywhere else. We then move them into a resourceful state, and while in this resourceful state, we take them back to the context where they used to experience the problem.

So why is it important to move the client's attention around like this? To answer this question, we need to look to at what we are now learning from a combination of neuroscience and quantum physics. Now, not being a neuroscientist or a quantum physicist, I will explain this concept in the easiest, most simplistic way possible.

Have you heard the expression "a watched pot never boils?" This theory is from quantum physics and is known as the Quantum Zeno Effect. The QZE states that the more a particle is observed, the less it changes. If we apply this concept to change work, we could say that "the more a client continues to focus on their issue, the more it stabilizes the problem and the less it changes." By intentionally moving the client's attention around to different things, we are beginning to "shake up the concrete" that has been holding the problem in place.

So one reason for continuously shifting the client's attention away from the problem and into something else is to begin to interrupt these patterns. We are literally interrupting the firing of the neural network. By interrupting it and redirecting it into new neural pathways, we are already beginning to rewire their brain for change.

A brief Neuroscientific Look at the Meta Pattern

The Meta Pattern is the simple 4-step process allowing the coach to elegantly use principles of state dependent learning, LTP and Hebb's Law, the 90-second rule and Neural Darwinism to create change in their clients.

Remember, the Meta Pattern is the structure of the change, not a pattern in of itself; we will be explaining how traditional NLP patterns fit into this structure. Let's explore the structure a little more fully and review some of the elements necessary for it to be effective within a neuroscientific context.

The Meta Pattern is the basis of HOW we do change work. It involves the coach intentionally moving the clients experience and attention through the 4 stages:

1. The Present State (the context, which will initially include the Problem State and behavior),

2. Dissociating from the Problem State,

3. Associating into the Resource State,

4. And the Resource State with the context both at the same time.

Think back to our brief example of Claudia and her fear of flying. By associating her into the fear, just dipping into it gently by asking her to think of flying, we will light up the correct neurological network for the context, including the problem feelings of fear. We just utilized Hebb's Law, lighting up the negative neural connection Claudia has made.

We ask how she wants to feel differently, but if we have not yet dissociated from the problem, then the only networks lighting up are those connected with the problem. Therefore all she can say is that she "doesn't want to feel afraid." In order for her to identify an appropriate resource, we first have to take her out of the Problem State using dissociation. Here we use the theory of the 90-second rule, purposefully interrupting the pattern Claudia had been running.

When she is dissociated from the context in which she normally experiences the problem, she is free to find an appropriate resource. Now of course the coach could simply guess at what the appropriate resource is; if she has been feeling fear, then perhaps the appropriate resource is confidence. We do not really agree with this approach (the coach choosing the resource for the client), but many coaches use it. Even if you do choose a resource for the client, in order for the client to actually feel that sense of confidence, the coach would still need to dissociate her from the fear.

Supposing we dissociate Claudia from the fear and ask her how she wants to feel instead. She says, "I want to feel calm." Later in the process, we get Claudia fully in touch with how it feels to be really calm, thus lighting up her "calm" neurological network, and helping to maintain and build this resource by allowing Claudia to turn it over and over in her mind, adding in more sensory information and using the state dependent learning theory to fully associate to this positive feeling.

The final step in the pattern is to begin to link these two together, utilizing Long Term Potentiation initially, which leads, through repetition, to these neurons becoming wired together (Hebb's Law).

We are lighting up ('collapsing') the "planes/flying/fear" network AT THE SAME TIME as the "calm" network. If we have made the "calm" network a big and robust enough resource, firing them all together is going to create a change. Repeating this 'collapse' a number of times strengthens the change until the feeling of calm overwhelms the feeling of fear, and a new default feeling is linked to the idea of flying. And of course the old neurological network that linked fear and flying is now severed (Neural Pruning).

By intentionally moving Claudia's attention around we have also utilized the Quantum Zeno Effect, which has helped Claudia to "shake up the concrete" in which the old problem was set and thereby make this change more easily.

Chapter Three:

The 4 steps of the Meta Pattern

In this chapter we will give an in-depth look at the four steps of this pattern. As you continue on, take a moment to think about the most influential or persuasive people and products you know. You will begin to notice these 4 steps as they naturally occur in your daily life. In fact, you may want to consider how you can apply them to your own life to create powerful change.

These steps are simple, and easy to remember. You may find it intriguing to realize that massive positive transformation is built into these 4 easy steps.

Although we refer to this as the Meta Pattern, it is not an NLP pattern; rather, it is the structure, the framework, upon which every pattern in NLP is built. Some people describe it as the foundation that supports change and upon which the NLP patterns and techniques are built. Others call it the umbrella under which all patterns lay. Whichever way you come to think of it, it is the intrinsic structure that runs though all NLP change techniques.

And not only that, this is such a fundamental pattern that it is easily utilized in business, sales, coaching, training and consulting. Whenever you want to help someone transform from where they currently are to someplace more resourceful, then this pattern is the key.

The Meta Pattern in Coaching

As coaches, it is our job to guide clients through navigating various states. We must have the ability to effortlessly move them from one state to the next so that transformation occurs. Of course, these state transitions are not random. We follow the pattern below so that no matter what is happening, we will always know where a client is at within the process of change. This also means that whatever response your client gives you is just the right response for you to use in the moment to create change. For example, a coach leads the client through a Swish and yet there is no physiological shift that would indicate a change in state. For the inexperienced coach, they may be happy to gloss over this fact, knowing something isn't right but afraid to address it in case they fail. Another coach, on the other hand, who understands these four steps, recognizes the lack of state change and knows the client is still in the Problem State and they have to work a bit harder to get the client into a resourceful state.

The Meta Pattern enables you to know always know how quickly your client is changing in 4 easy steps:

1. Associate into context of the Present or Problem State

2. Dissociate from the Problem State

3. Associate into a Resourceful State

4. Take the new Resource State back to the context of Problem State. This causes both the Resource and Problem States to be present at the same time, and hence collapses the problem into the resource.

We will be talking in detail about how to do each of these steps using any of the NLP, hypnosis or coaching patterns that you may know later in the book. For now, we will simply gives a brief overview of each of the steps.

Associating into the Context of the Problem

Sometimes it will be extremely easy to associate the client into the problem. They will already be in it! For example, if a client comes to your office with anxiety, they may be feeling anxious when they walk in!

You may also be able to trigger the Problem State in the client. For example, when we see clients who want to stop smoking, we say to them, "Smoke your last cigarette the evening before you come to the session!" This generally makes it fairly easy to associate them into the Problem State of 'wanting a cigarette,' so that we can show them how to deal with cravings. Incidentally, if they don't have a craving for a cigarette (and they followed the instruction not to smoke since the previous evening), it proves to them that they can stop smoking without experiencing cravings.

Sometimes it may not be so obvious how to associate the client into the context of the problem. For example, if a client comes with a fear of speaking to large groups, it is unlikely that you will have a large group of people in your office that they can speak to in order to generate this fear. But remember, the unconscious mind is not able to differentiate between reality and something that is strongly imagined. As long as you can get them to imagine they are speaking in front of a large group, this will be enough to associate them into the context of speaking to a large group, and hence to trigger the fear.

We will be talking more about various techniques to associate the clients back into the context of the Problem State in a later chapter.

Dissociating the client

The main reason for dissociating the clients from the problem, and from the negative feelings which the problem generates, is so that they can find a suitable Resource State. When they are in the Problem State, it may be that everything is colored by that state. For example, let's return to the client who comes in with a fear of speaking in public, and instead they want to feel confident. If you associate them into the fear, the chances are they will not be able to find a sense of confidence until the fear has left.

There are many ways of dissociating the client from the Present State that we will be talking about later. For now, just be aware that it will be very difficult to get the client to think, feel and behave resourcefully as long as they are in the Problem State.

Associating into a Resource

But before we begin talking about how to associate your clients into a more resourceful state, we should briefly discuss what a state is. A state can be thought of as an emotional state, such as a state of confidence, but it's much more than just the emotion. A state impacts on everything about the person, from their physiology, how they hold their body and how they gesture, their breathing, but also things like their beliefs and values, what they believe about themselves and the world around them, and what is important to them at that time.

Consider the client who has a fear of speaking in public and wants to feel confident instead. While in a state of fear, they probably believe things like, "I can't do this," and they probably have 'away-from' values such as safety. In contrast, when in a state of confidence, his belief will change to, "I can do this," and his values may shift to include things such as 'sharing information.'

Will be talking a lot more about how to select an appropriately resourceful state for the client, and how to associate them into this state, later in the book. It turns out that it is the same method that we use to associate the client into the context of the problem; the unconscious mind cannot tell the difference between reality and something that is strongly imagined. By tapping into the client's imagination, suitable resources can normally be found fairly easily.

Collapsing the Problem Context with the Resourceful State

We have come onto the fourth and final step in the Meta Pattern, collapsing the problem with the resource. Remember the key to coaching is not just being able to take your client into a resourceful feeling, but making sure that that resourceful feeling is available to them when they need it. And when they need it is the precise context in which they want to change, the context in which they previously experienced the problem.

By taking them into the new resourceful state and asking them to imagine they are in the context in which they previously experienced the problem, we light up the two circuits at the same time: the context and the resource. LTP (see the chapter on neuroscience) takes over and these two circuits become sensitized to each other. Run the pattern enough times by simultaneously lighting up 'context' and 'resource,' and Hebb's Law takes over; two circuits become permanently wired together, and the client will feel confident (or whatever the resourceful state is) the next time they are speaking to a group (or whatever the context is).

Whatever NLP, hypnosis or coaching pattern you are using, if you want to guarantee that Hebb's Law will wire the circuits together, you need to have emotional intensity by boosting the resourceful state as much as possible and making the experience fun, as well as using repetition.

The Meta Pattern and Influence

Everything that we said above about using the Meta Pattern in coaching applies equally if we are using the Meta Pattern in business, sales, storytelling or making a speech. We will be talking about these individually in later chapters, but we will offer a teaser here.

The first step of the Meta Pattern is to associate into the context of the problem. It really doesn't matter whether you are in business, selling a widget, selling an idea, selling yourself on a job interview, selling a story to an audience, selling your political views to a constituency, or your spiritual views to a congregation. The first thing that you have to do is to let your audience know "what's in it for me?" If they don't see the personal benefit in what you have to say, they just won't listen. This is sometimes referred to as selling the benefits not features, or selling the sizzle not the steak.

To do this, you have to remind the audience of a problem they are experiencing, or point out to them what they are missing out on (a life bereft of joy because they do not own your product), or a problem that someone else is facing in a story or parable that they can identify with.

The second step of the Meta Pattern is to disassociate them from the context of the problem. Generally, you will do this by giving them information; information about your product, information about a journey the character in the story undertakes, or statistical information that supports your political case. Whatever type of information it is, it is designed to get them to begin thinking rather than feeling. While they are taking in the information and thinking about it, their neurology and physiology has the required '90 seconds' to reset.

48

The third step in the Meta Pattern is to associate them into the resource. You can do this by inviting them to imagine how their life will be once they have bought your product, voted for you, accepted your invitation for a date, or whatever else you are proposing to them. The more intensely they can imagine this, the more deeply they will feel the associated emotional state. In the case of a story, the Resource State will be some experience that the hero of the story has.

The final step in the Meta Pattern is the collapse. If you're selling a product or an idea, the collapse will be all about how they can continue to feel the positive feelings you just showed them. For example, you may ask them to sign on the dotted line! In the case of a story, the final step of the story is where the hero takes the lessons she has learned and somehow returns to the everyday world of experience.

Chapter Four:

Association and Dissociation

Association

Association is one of those words that has become overused in NLP. It has several slightly different, but related, meanings depending upon the context. For example, in the context of the visual sense, association is used as a visual 'submodality'; you are said to be associated into a picture you are making in your mind if you are 'looking out of your own eyes.' In contrast, you are said to be dissociated if you see yourself in the picture.

In contrast, in the context of feelings, the kinesthetic sense, we say that someone is 'associated' into a state when they are experiencing it, and experiencing it to the fullest extent. It is as though they have stepped into the experience so completely that to all intents and purposes they are 'there.'

Now, when someone is associated in the visual sense (seeing out of their own eyes), they are more likely to be associated in the kinesthetic sense, feeling the emotions that go along with that context. So, for the rest of this book, when we talk about association, we will be implying that the person is seeing, hearing and feeling what they would have been seeing, hearing and feeling at the appropriate time and context. It is like they are reliving it, bringing it to life so the experience feels very real.

We can also associate into another person's experience by imagining we are them, that we are seeing out of their eyes, hearing with their ears, and experiencing their emotions. In NLP this possibility is explored in perceptual position work, as well as in techniques like the new behavior generator.

And we can associate into memories from the past, imagined scenes, and into future events.

Associating into an Experience Using Revivification

How can we associate someone into a state or experience? The easiest way to do this is to ask, "When was the last time you experienced this?... Where are you? What's happening?" The key here is for us to begin to use present tense language in order to bring the event to life in the fullest sense. If someone us speaking in the past tense or telling us about the experience, then they are not associated. It is the job of the change worker to move the client into becoming associated and to hold them there...maintain the association until we need to change.

For example, lets say that Phil is telling us about a birthday party he attended a few years back. Note how the coach gently moves into present tense and helps Phil to maintain the association to feel the same way he felt then, in the here and now:

Phil: It was such a great party. We were all outside around the pool.

Coach: That sounds fantastic, so you are all outside around the pool...tell me more...what are you seeing?

Phil: I can see Jim at the barbecue and Jenna is bringing out the corn for Jim to grill.

Coach: Sounds delicious, what's happening now?

Phil: Well, the kids are playing in the pool and Jenna is calling them to come and watch us open the presents.

Coach: And how are you feeling right now?

Phil: I am feeling fantastic and really happy being with my family.

Association using Pacing and Leading

Pacing and leading is an NLP technique that allows the coach to lead the client in a certain direction in small incremental steps. Because each step is small, it is a very simple and easy way to lead a client into a positive state, and because many different steps can be used, the state can be extremely powerful. Pacing and leading can be combined with the revivification technique described above, but it can also be used by itself.

Here is an example of how small steps can be used to create a large state; let's say the state is confidence. Consider each question carefully before moving onto the next:

What's it like when you're feeling confident?

Where in your body do you feel that feeling of confidence? Is it on the inside (of your body), or the outside? Where does the feeling of confidence start? Where does it move to next?

As you feel that sense of confidence, notice the size and shape of the feeling. What happens if you increase the size of the feeling?

Notice if the feeling is moving. For example, is it spinning in one direction or another? If it is, what happens if you spin it a little faster, or a little slower?

Is there a color of your feeling of confidence? I know this is a strange question, but fully consider it now. If there is a color, what happens if you make it brighter?

Asking questions of this sort allows a positive feeling or state to be slowly built up and magnified.

Here's another example from a coaching session:

Coach: How do you want to feel that's different to how you've been feeling?

Client: I want to feel confident.

Coach: And what is it like when you're feeling confident?

Client: I'm not sure.

Coach: As you're feeling confident now, where do you feel that?

Client: I guess I feel it in my chest.

Coach: That's right, you feel it in your chest. Whereabouts in your chest do you feel it?

Client: It's here, right in the middle.

Coach: Is there a size or shape of confidence as you're feeling it there, in the middle of your chest?

Client: Is like a golden ball, the size of a baseball.

Coach: So it's like a golden ball, the size of a baseball, and is it moving? I notice your hand is turning…

Client: Yes, it's spinning.

Coach: And what happens if you spin it a little faster…

And so on. You will notice that the coach repeats back what the client is just said. This is the 'pacing' part of the pacing and leading. In NLP it is sometimes called 'backtracking.' Once the coach has helped to 'fix' that piece of the client's experience by repeating it back, the coach then asks for more pieces of clarifying information which is then added to the puzzle. By approaching the resource in this incremental way, the resource can be powerfully built up.

Association = fully in the experience

Dissociation

In NLP, dissociation is the opposite of association. So when you make a picture in your mind, and rather than looking out of your own eyes, you see yourself in the picture, you are said to be dissociated in respect to the picture. Dissociation is therefore a visual 'submodality.'

In respect of feelings, dissociation is when I am not actually feeling the emotion I'm talking about or thinking about. For example, if I'm talking about a time when I got extremely angry, but I'm talking about that experience in a very calm and measured way, that I am dissociated from the feeling of anger.

Some people dissociate more easily than others. They become emotional less often than the average. As an example, think of Mr. Spock from *Star Trek*.

So to be dissociated from a state means to be apart from it, distanced and almost like an observer without any feeling or emotion attached. Very often when someone is dissociated, they are able to see themselves in the scene...almost like a 'fly on the wall' with no emotional attachment to it.

Other times, we are able to dissociate from an event or experience by fully paying attention to anything that is NOT the event. To help someone dissociate from a memory or experience, we can simply ask them to tell us about anything other than the event, or ask them to get up and move around, or ask them a very cognitive question that will make them stop and think hard about something.

Easy examples of this would be:

"So tell me about your hobby of horseback riding, Phil."

Or

"Phil, I would like you to come and stand over here and raise your right arm to about shoulder height."

Or

"What is your telephone number backwards?"

These are known in NLP terms as classic "Break States." They are an intentional question or instruction to the client to shift their awareness and move it towards something else entirely. These are 'hard' breaks where we are directing the client's mind into an alternative pathway, often utilizing a sense that they had not previously been using. For example, If a client is talking about feeling less than resourceful and we can see that they are talking themselves further into feeling bad, we may use a break state to dissociate them and at the same time direct them toward a sense that they had not been using. Here's an example:

Otis: And it seems that every time I see my boss's face I just get so scared that she is going to fire me. I am getting all hot and I feel like I am tight inside.

Coach: Hey, Otis…do you smell popcorn?

Otis: What?…(sniffing) Nope…but that sounds like a good idea!

Another way to do this is to ask the client to imagine seeing themselves, making a picture of the event and simply observing how that are behaving, standing breathing etc. Again, it is the change worker's role to ensure that the client maintains this distance and is able to talk about him or herself in the third person:

Otis: And it seems that every time I see my boss's face I just get so scared that she is going to fire me. I am getting all hot and I feel like I am tight inside.

Coach: OK… so now as you step over here I want you to look back at that Otis over there and tell me what you see.

Otis: Well… I am….

Coach: He… is…

Otis: Oh, right…he is standing by his desk and he is a bit hunched over.

Coach: How is he breathing?

Otis: He seems to be breathing a bit shallow.

Dissociation = distanced from the experience.

Using Association and Dissociation in Coaching

Being able to associate and dissociate clients into and out of different experiences and to hold them in either one is absolutely key for change work. This is often how a client is making himself or herself feel unresourceful because they are associating too fully into negative states or are complexly distanced from any feelings. Our role is to be able to elegantly shift our clients through different experiences so as to guide and direct the change.

Chapter Five:

Step 1: Associating into the Context of the Problem

The first step of the Meta Pattern is to associate the client into the context of the problem. At first this may sound counterintuitive; after all, if your client comes to you for help, why would you take him back to the thing that's bothering him? Why would we want them to relive it, to step inside it? If it is an undesirable state, surely asking them to bring it back to life will be uncomfortable and possibly cause them unnecessary stress? The answer of course lays in the neuroscience. Any change requires that we wire a new resource to the old problem circuitry, and to do this we first have to identify the circuitry to be rewired. We have to light up the problem.

The fact is that your client is probably associating into their problem on a pretty regular basis on his own. That's why he considers it to be a problem! He doesn't want to be feeling the way he feels when he associates back into that context, but he doesn't know how to resolve it (after all, if he did he would have solved it for himself without the need to come and visit you!).

Associating the client into their problem does several other things for us. First it gives us, the change worker, an opportunity to calibrate how the client appears and behaves when he is in his problem. This gives us a baseline upon which to easily see when a shift or change has happened. This also acts as a convincer for the client to be aware of his change. When we point out how he feels in our office, while accessing the problem, and then revisit how he feels after we have run through the change pattern, asking him to "notice how it is different now," it helps him to begin to observe the differences, subtle and not so subtle, in how he feels about the context of the problem.

Secondly, associating the client into the problem and using our calibration skills also helps us to begin to figure out exactly HOW the client is doing their problem. Let's take Claudia again.

Claudia comes into my office with a drastic fear of flying. I don't have to do a great deal of work to associate her into the problem because as soon as she begins to talk about an upcoming flight she has to take, her fingers begin to clench, her voice tone shifts and becomes tight, and she says she can feel her stomach churn.

As she dips into this state, I notice her eyes flick up and to her right. I ask her, "What picture can you see up there?" At first Claudia looks a little unsure and says she can just see my hand pointing to the space. When I ask her to look more closely, she looks startled and says, "Oh my goodness, I am seeing a picture of a newscast telling of a plane crash!"

"How's that working out for you?" I ask (a little tongue in cheek).

"It's horrible," she says. "I have been scaring myself by making these awful pictures, and I didn't even know it."

Claudia's unconscious mind had been providing her with many nasty images that were fueling her fear of flying. No wonder she was feeling terrible.

In order for us to be effective, we need to be very specific with the network we are lighting up. We will ask the client to select a very specific time and place when the problem occurs. A client may come in and say, "Oh, it happens all the time," and you as the coach can say, "That's great, tell me about just one time!" Problems generalize easily...this is often how they have manifested to begin with; Johnny only had to have a few times when he felt anxious while performing for his brain to wire the network together. So it really does appear to be happening "every time" or "always."

How Do We Associate into the Problem State?

So how do we do this? Remember back to our discussion about association? The easiest and quickest way to associate into a state is to ask your client to begin to describe one time they had the problem. As they begin to describe it, you will begin to lead them into describing it in the present tense. The tense shifts have been italicized to make them clear to you. For example:

Nate: I always get so nervous when I have to make a presentation and I just want to stop.

Coach: OK, so you get nervous when making a presentation and you just want to stop.

Nate: Yeah, it's awful.

Coach: OK, so tell me about the last time and place you remember doing this.

Nate: Well, it happens every Monday morning because I have to make a presentation to my department colleagues.

Coach: OK, so pick one Monday to focus on specifically.

Nate: OK, well just yesterday.

Coach: What time *is* the meeting?

Nate: About 9.

Coach: And where *are you?*

Nate: In the conference room at work.

Coach: Ok so it *is yesterday around 9 o'clock and you are in the conference room*

Nate: Mmmm.

Coach: Where *is* the light coming from?

Nate: There are windows to my right

Coach: OK so *it is Monday, around 9 o'clock and you are in the conference room at work and what are you doing?*

Nate: I am listening to my boss and thinking that it is my turn next and I am feeling my heart begin to race and my stomach is churning.

Coach: Ahh.

So in this example, just a shift in tense was able to take Nate back to the previous day and hold him there while he began to relive exactly how he was starting to do his problem. You will also notice that the coach repeats the exact phrases that Nate uses. The helps to stabilize the context and to revivify the experience and at the same time it is ensuring that there is rapport between coach and client. It feels very comfortable to hear your exact words mirrored back, so it is important to use the client's precise words.

Asking for specific times and details like "where is the light coming from?" helps to associate the client even more fully into the experience.

Sometimes it is necessary to give even more direction to the client so they know exactly what is being asked of them. I could have said something like:

"So what I would like you to do, Nate, is to go back yesterday in the conference room and really step into as though you are reliving it completely, seeing what you see, hearing what you hear and feeling what you are feeling."

From here I could continue to ask Nate to describe what is happening and maintain his association into the Problem State.

Sometimes a client will come into the office and they are already associated into their problem. They will likely be speaking in the present tense and demonstrating the behaviors associated with their issue. When this happens, there is no need to spend time associating them into the problem because they are already there! We may want to help them focus on one specific example of the problem to ensure that we are lighting up exactly the correct neurological network.

Why do we pick a particular example?

You will also notice in the above example that I ask Nate for a particular example, a very specific time and place when the problem has occurred. This helps him to associate into just one time, and lights up the exact neurological network associated with the issue. This is vitally important, as we need to know exactly where, neurologically speaking, to attach the resource.

There is another very important aspect to consider here too. If we think back to HOW a problem is generated and generalized, it usually happens one incident at a time. An initial incident is followed by a few more incidents that generalize into "I always feel this way." Of course, there can be cases when there is a very strong emotional response and the problem/fear/worry arises from that one incident, but in general we need to begin to make the changes in the same way, the same manner, one event at a time. If we do, the same principle of generalization will occur, only this time it will generalize to the solution.

Trying to solve the big overall issue in one go is like trying to eat the whole elephant…it's just impossible! Bite-sized pieces are the way to go and the unconscious mind very quickly will understand what to do.

As we have said, if a client says, "It happens all the time," it's great because it offers lots of events to pick from. The key here is to keep the client entirely focused on the one time they select and not allow them to jump to a new event before the first event has been cleared. Once we have cycled through the Meta Pattern a few times if necessary (using whichever patterns you like) and have a change, then we ask the client to select another specific time and place and go through that one as well. Then we ask them to pick a third event and so on, until they are unable to find any more. Usually, by the time we have changed 3 or 4 or 5 events, the client is unable to find any others that have the same emotional impact, even though they previously stated that "it happens all the time." The unconscious mind has generalized the change quickly and efficiently.

How do we know if they are Associated into the Problem State?

So we know the issue we are working through with the client, we have narrowed it down to just one specific time and place, and are asking the client to step back into the experience fully and completely, associating them into it using present tense language.

But how do we know if the client is really fully associated into the Problem State? In order for us to be able to help the client to change, they need to be feeling the Problem State just enough so that we know that the correct and neurological network has been fired. The client needs to "feel it to heal it." So we are looking for physiological signs from the client to let us know that they are feeling a little bit of the Problem State. We need to calibrate to how the client is looking, their tone of voice, what their posture is like, and to any gestures they may be using. We are looking for any shift such as a flush of the skin, a sigh or alteration in the tone or speed of their speech, a change in breathing or in their physical stance or posture.

The body is usually the first to 'speak' and it is essential that we have part of us following along with the client's story and another part of us following along with any and all shifts in the physicality of the client. Some clients will dip into the Problem State and demonstrate it very clearly, whereas others have less outward affect. If I am not seeing any kind of shift, I will usually step in and directly ask the client, "How do you know, in your body, that you are feeling X?" This directs the client's attention to scan their body and find the physical sensation associated with the issue or problem.

What do we do if we can't Associate them into the Context of the Problem and the Problem State?

If the client has difficulty associating into the problem, there are a few things that we can do to help them. One way is to ask them to make a movie of the specific time and place. We ask the client to imagine watching him or herself in the movie (this would be dissociated), and to make it life-size. Once the image is life-size, we ask the client to imagine that they can 'step in' to the movie and become the 'you,' to fully experience it, seeing what they see, hearing what they hear, and feeling what they are feeling. This often helps someone to associate into an event; it's a little bit like a stepping-stone and makes the association easier for the client.

What do we do if we really can't Associate them into the Context of the Problem and the Problem State?

Sometimes it can prove extremely difficult to associate the client into the problem. And we mean really difficult.

Client: I get terrified when I have to fly.

Coach: When was the last time this happened?

Client: It was last week. I had to fly to Detroit.

Coach: So you're getting on the airplane, how are you feeling?... You're sitting in your seat, how are you feeling?... The plane is taking off, how are you feeling?... There is turbulence, how are you feeling?

For each question, the client answers, "I'm not feeling anything."

In this case, it proves extremely difficult to associate the client into any sort of state; it is worth asking yourself what the client's actual problem is…

Coach: Let me show you a technique to deal with unwanted feelings, like your fear of flying. But first we'll change something easy first. Tell me about the last time you were angry or frustrated…

Client: I was driving here in traffic, and it was frustrating.

Coach: So you are driving in traffic, and you're feeling frustrated, where in your body are you feeling that?

Client: I'm not feeling that.

Coach: Ah. If you could feel any way you want to feel, right now, how will that be? How will you be feeling?

Client: I don't want to feel anything. I want to feel nothing.

In this case, the client's problem is not necessarily her fear of flying (although of course this may be a real problem for her), but her desire to be dissociated from her feelings. This could be symptomatic of some deeper issue.

Chapter Six: Step 2:

Dissociating from the Problem State

Why Do We Dissociate the Client?

Once the client has associated into the problem and we have clearly seen how they are when in the problem, and we have some insight into how they are doing the problem, e.g. making pictures, telling themselves nasty things, and so on, it is time to disassociate them. Remember, we only keep the client in the negative, Problem State for as brief a time as necessary for us to gather all the information we need and for the correct neurological network to have been lit up. This is also beginning to utilize the Quantum Zeno effect of the need to shift attention in order to make a change!

Most of us have, at one time or another, felt un-resourceful or down in the dumps. When we are feeling this way, it is really difficult to look for a better way to feel. We have probably all experienced feeling down and somebody saying, "Look on the bright side," or "Just snap out of it" or something along those lines. What usually happens when we hear this? Does it help? Not usually; it may make you mutter something under your breath at the person, as you feel misunderstood.

When we are feeling a certain way it is as though we have special glasses on that filter for similar feelings and experiences. John Overdurf says, "We sort by states." This means that when we are feeling unhappy, it is easier for us to find other times and experiences when we felt equally unhappy. And it is harder for us to find more positive ways of feeling. With this in mind, we can clearly see the need to dissociate our client from their negative state. We need to help them to find any state/feeling or emotion other than the one associated with their problem.

How do we Dissociate from the Problem State?

We can help somebody to dissociate from the problem in a number of ways. A very quick and easy way to break the state is to ask the client a totally unrelated question. The client is likely to be in their Problem State, seeing or hearing something related to the problem and feeling something unpleasant. A classic NLP 'break state' question is to ask, "Do you smell popcorn?" By asking this question, we are shifting the client's awareness to the sense of smell, intentionally moving their sensory awareness away from whatever it was they were seeing, hearing and feeling, by moving them into the sense of smell. By changing the sensory mode, we are moving the client's awareness to a totally new area.

We could also ask and unrelated question about what's the client is wearing, what they had for lunch, or any other question which will draw the attention away from the problem. We always ask (on our intake form) about any hobbies or pastimes the client has. This gives us lots of scope to ask the client about something they enjoy doing, thus changing their thought patterns and dissociation them from the negative.

Asking the client a very 'left brain' type of question is another way to dissociate them from the problem. You might ask them to tell you their telephone number backwards, or give them in mathematical problem to solve (unless they have a math phobia!).

Another way to dissociate a client from a negative state is to ask them to change their physiology. Asking them to stand up, to move to a different chair, or to write something down will also shift them out of the negative state.

Laughter is a wonderful state to get the client into. People who laugh at their problems don't have problems; they just have jokes and comedy in their lives. We want our client to be laughing at something within the first 10 minutes of walking in the door. By doing this, we are already creating, and of course anchoring, a state that is a great dissociative state, and one from which they will be able to move easily into an appropriate resource.

Now, we are not suggesting that you need to be a comedian (although it may help), and with certainly not suggesting that you laugh at the client's problem (although some very successful therapists do). However, there are many ways to naturally bring laughter into the session. I know of a change worker who will simply cross her legs and, while doing so, tap the client's shin or foot. When she does this she says, "Oh sorry!" and giggles a bit. Within a few moments she does it again giggles some more, saying sorry once again. By this time the client is also giggling. It is a very natural and easy way to get a little bit of laughter. Of course, now each and every time she bumps the client's leg, there will be laughter. We suggest that you find ways to bring a giggle, a smile and laughter into your sessions. The more you repeat the action or phrase, the more it becomes linked to laughter and becomes an anchor for dissociation. This is a very easy way to dissociate your client from any negative state.

When I asked Claudia about the nasty pictures she was making in her mind, I said, with a twinkle in my eye, "How's that's working out for you?" and she began to smile at herself as she began to realize what she had been doing unconsciously to make herself feel bad. This simple yet effective question will often lead to the same response. Of course, it has to be asked with a 'twinkle in the eye' and in exquisite rapport, because we are gently teasing our client. But if we can get our client to begin to laugh at his or her own problem, then we are well on the road towards change.

One important technique as the coach is to shift your voice tone and body language when shifting the client's state. We communicate not only with our words but also through our tonality and physiology. By ensuring that we, the change worker, have shifted into a new state will help to lead the client out of the negative state and into this 'intermediate' break-state, or dissociation. It is a great idea to find your own jokes funny (even if nobody else does!); if you can't make them laugh *with* you, you can at least get them to laugh *at* you. Our teacher John Overdurf calls this a "pity laugh," but it still counts!

Another favorite dissociation technique of ours, which we learned from our teacher Melissa Tiers, is to simply say, "Stop!" with an emphatic tone while raising our palm in front of the client's face. This can appear to be a very abrupt technique, and indeed that is its intention. After we've done this technique the first time, to soften this a little I usually say something like:

"I'm sorry, that must've appeared rude. However, part of my job as coach is to interrupt your negative patterns. Each time I do this, it begins to literally rewire your brain for change." I then go on to explain what I mean. I will tell the client that their unconscious mind has created a pathway in the brain that leads from the trigger, whatever sets them off (thinking about an upcoming flight, feeling a roughness on their nails, etc.) to the negative feeling or behavior. This route has become very well used, almost like a super highway. This is why they feel that they have no control and that the problem happens all the time. My job is to put a 'stop sign' along the route and to begin to create an alternative way, another pathway that leads to a better outcome, a nicer feeling and a more resourceful behavior. I explain that we might have to do this a number of times. I then give the client another metaphor to say, something like this:

"It's like we are creating an new pathway in the forest. At first you are changing track; you may have to cut through the trees and the vegetation. The second time it is a little easier already, and by the third or fourth time you can see the pathway more clearly. Soon you have created a roadway and then you have created a new superhighway to feeling good now. And of course we all know what happens in a forest to the pathway that is no longer walked down… that's right… it becomes overgrown and impassible very quickly. And this is exactly what is happening on the neurological basis too, so every time I say stop and raise my hand, we are helping your brain to create a new neurological pathway for you."

I find that clients respond remarkably well to this. It has a clear and easy metaphor that they can understand backed up with a more scientific explanation of what is happening inside their brain.

Clients are often very used to telling their story, either to others or themselves. Their story has become part of their identity, something that they *are*. It has become an unconscious pattern that runs very easily. What we are doing here by abruptly stopping their story is intentionally interrupting this unconscious pattern. This is known in NLP as a Pattern Interrupt and is a great way to dissociate the client from the Problem State.

We are utilizing two concepts here: Hebb's Law ("neurons that fire together wire together") and Neural Darwinism, the idea of "use it or lose it." Current research into neuroplasticity shows that our brains have the capacity to rewire themselves, to create new pathways and to change physical structure. The idea is that the more we repeat certain actions, the stronger the connections are within the brain. On the flip side of this, according to Gerald Edelman and his Neural Darwinism theory, when brain circuits or networks are not used, they the will begin to weaken and can be lost altogether. Both of these are being used within the Meta Pattern and I have found that my clients love to have a scientific reason for why we are doing what we are doing. So let's continue on with Nate as our example. Remember, we have already associated Nate into the problem:

Coach: OK, so it is Monday, around 9 o'clock and you are in the conference room at work, and what are you doing?

Nate: I am listening to my boss and thinking that it is my turn next and I am feeling my heart begin to race and my stomach is churning.

Coach: Ahh.

Nate: ...and I am saying "oh it's my turn soon" and I am feeling so...

Coach: Just stop there, Nate (raising my hand as I speak and changing my voice tone). Oh, I'm sorry. I don't mean to be rude, but it is my job to interrupt this pattern that you have been running and to begin to help you to redirect towards a more resourceful way of being. You see, it's like you have created a superhighway from the situation in the conference room to feeling nervous. It has become so very habitual to you that it probably seems like the two things have become one, and that every time you have to present, these feelings just happen (nodding my head to hopefully lead Nate into nodding his head and therefore demonstrating unconscious agreement).

Nate: (nodding his head) Yep.

Coach: So what we are doing here is putting up a 'roadblock' on that superhighway and redirecting your mind to take a new, better, more resourceful pathway through the forest that will lead you toward feeling the way you want to feel.

Nate: Great.

Coach: Now, because we are creating an new pathway in the forest, the first time you are changing track you may have to cut through the trees and the vegetation. The second time it is a little easier already, and by the third or fourth time you can see the pathway more clearly. Soon you have created a roadway and then you have created a new superhighway to feeling good now. And of course we all know what happens in a forest to the pathway that is no longer walked down… that's right… it becomes overgrown and impassible very quickly. And this is exactly what is happening on the neurological basis too, so every time I say stop and raise my hand, we are helping your brain to create a new neurological pathway for you, leading you to feeling great.

This process has done a number of things for Nate. Firstly, it has dissociated him from the problem and given him a great metaphor to understand why we are interrupting like this and a reason why we may loop through this pattern or similar ones a few times

How do we know if they are Dissociated?

All this time, we are calibrating and observing our client to ensure that they have dissociated from the problem. We will be looking for any physiological shift from the client. This may include a change in skin tone, voice tone, breathing, posture, gestures, head tilt, voice tempo or pitch. Any of these demonstrate to us that there has been a shift away from the state. If we combine these with the words the client is saying, we will get a clear visual picture that something has already changed.

As coach, you need a kind of 'split attention' where one part of you tracks exactly what the client is saying while at the same time we are also tracking and noticing physiological changes.

Another way to check that the client has dissociated from the problem, and one that naturally leads into step three of the Meta Pattern, is by asking them how they want to be instead. If they are still associated into the problem, they are likely to say something like, "I don't want to feel anxious [or whatever the problem is]." Whereas if they are more dissociated, they will state their answer in a positive, perhaps something like, "I want to be confident."

What do we do if we can't Dissociate them?

Occasionally it is a bit of a challenge to dissociate the client from the problem. When this happens, I find the very best way to dissociate the client is to physically move them, to ask them to stand up, shake off the problem, perhaps to move to another part of the room. Watch out for positive changes in their physiology such as a straightening of the spine, lifting of the head, more symmetrical gestures, more eye contact and so on.

Sometimes you'll find that you can dissociate the client from the problem, but they almost immediately drop back into it. This is a great time to use the more 'in your face' Interrupts such as, "Stop!" You can repeat this pattern interrupt a number of times to really start diverging their neural pathways.

Very occasionally you'll come across a client who will resent your interrupts, even when you have explained the reason for them. They will simply enjoy telling the story so much that they want to share it with you again and again and again. There are couple of great techniques for dealing with this:

We learned this from our teacher John Overdurf, who was working with a client who was herself a therapist and seemed to revel in explaining the deep-seated reasons for her having her problem. John reframes this by saying something like, "When you make this change, when you get rid of this issue, you'll have a great story to share." This allowed the client to keep the benefits of having a great story, while still obtaining the change she desired.

Another technique we learned from Nick Kemp, a wonderful therapist from the UK who specializes in Provocative Therapy. When a client walks in to see him, and he knows they are going to want to tell him that story over and over again (either because he has seen it before, or because he makes them fill out an extensive intake questionnaire before they come to see him), he will say something like, "Thank God it's you. I just had a session with a client who went on and on and on about their problem. I simply couldn't get them to stop. It's amazing that people like that come to see me saying they want to change, but all they really want to do is talk about that problem. How can you change, when all you talk about is your problems? Now, what you want to work through?" This sort of approach is called a pre-frame, and effectively inoculates your client against this sort of 'problem storytelling.'

As a last resort, you can simply challenge them: "You can begin to consider what you actually want, how you actually want to feel, or, you can continue to focus on, and talk about, your problem. The choice is yours. If you must talk about your problem, you can go and see a talk-therapist for the next 10 years; they'll be happy to listen. Now, what do you want to change, and how do you want to be different?" This is obviously a very direct approach that may break your client out of their habitual pattern, or may cause them to go and see a talk therapist instead!

Chapter Seven:

Step 3: Associating into the Resource State

What is a Resource State?

Once the client is dissociated from the problem, it is time to shift their attention towards how they would like to be feeling and acting. In NLP terms, this is known as a Resource State. A Resource State is a positive state from where they can be more in control, make better choices, and take better actions. It is usually a state that feels good, although states such as anger can be resources in the right context.

It is important that this state is one that the client describes in the positive, for example, "I want to feel calm," or "I would like to feel focused and energized." Occasionally, when asked how they would like to feel, a client will answer in the negative, for example, "I don't want to feel nervous." When this happens, it is essential that we recognize this and steer them towards stating their outcome positively by saying something like, "And when you are not feeling nervous, how are you feeling?"

The Resource State also has to be something that is within the client's own control, an internal state that is not dependent upon what somebody else does, or happens outside. Sometimes a client will say they want their boss/partner/child/etc. to stop or start behaving in a certain way, or to stop "making me feel that way." For example, "I would like for Cindy to stop shouting at me." In reality, the only person that we have control over is ourselves, so I would ask the client to reconsider, "Yes that would be nice, but you know that the only person you can really control is yourself, so with that in mind and given the fact that Cindy may continue to shout…how would you like to be feeling?"

Once the client has identified how they would like to be feeling, we are ready to associate them into this feeling, in the here and now; again, they need to light up the specific neurological network associated with their resourceful state.

How do we Associate them into the Resource State?

To associate the client into the resource, we use exactly the same principles of association that we discussed before. For example, we can find an example of when they felt/feel the resource, and begin to use present tense language to step into it fully and completely.

We can do this is a number of ways. Some coaches believe that they have to find a time in the past when the client was feeling that resourceful feeling. This isn't necessarily true, nor is it always the simplest way. In fact, as soon as the client has said how she would like to feel, perhaps "confident," we can ask:

"And what's it like when you are as you are feeling confident…and as you are feeling confident now, notice how you are standing…how you are breathing…what you are believing about yourself?"

As soon as she mentions the specific Resource State, her brain is literally beginning to fire the connections associated with that resource. By switching into present tense language, particularly works such as "feeling," "believing" and other "-ing" words, (i.e. present progressive tense), we begin to build up the physiological responses that accompany it, the positive beliefs that it includes, and any other associations it may have.

Of course we could ask them about a specific time and place that they felt this resourceful state, and then begin to associate them into the experience using present tense language shifts.

For example, Nate has to make a presentation at the Monday morning meeting each week and he gets nervous whenever he thinks about it. When asked how he would like to feel, he says he wants to feel calm when presenting. We will focus just on the 'associating into the resource' for this example:

Coach: So when was the last time and place you were feeling really calm?

Nate: About 6 months ago.

Coach: Where were you?

Nate: On the beach in Puerto Rico.

Coach: Ooohh lovely, so you are on the beach in Puerto Rico, are you on a lounger, sitting on the sand…what are you doing?

Nate: I am lying on the sun lounger and feeling the sun on my skin.

Coach: And as you are lying there and feeling the sun on your skin, how is the rest of your body feeling now?

Nate: Really relaxed and calm.

We are calibrating again for the physiological shifts and changes in the client (breathing, color changes, expression, voice tone, etc.) to let us know that they have fully associated into the resourceful state.

Another essential factor to helping a client associate into their resource is for the coach to take on the aspects of the resource themselves. When I was working with Nate and he said he wanted to feel calm, I immediately shifted my voice tone and began to say the word calm in the most relaxed, calm way possible. I also shifted in my chair, leaned back, stretched out my legs a bit and let my shoulders relax. I accessed a state of calmness in order to non-verbally demonstrate 'calm' and to lead Nate into that state more easily. We have mirror neurons in our brains that fire off when we observe a behavior; it is almost as though we are 'trying on' the behavior inside our mind, and this can manifest on the outside too. Have you ever watched a sports fan watch a very intense game? They are likely to be moving slightly in the same way as the athletes, mirroring and copying the behaviors they are observing. The exact same things happen to a client when we begin to model the resources they wish to access. For years, the change work community has been saying that the coach needs to "go first," whether into trance when hypnotizing a client, or into the resourceful state, and now there is scientific evidence to support why this works so wonderfully well!

Once the client has accessed this positive feeling or state, we can begin to enhance it and build it up to make it stronger and an even bigger resource for them. There are a few ways we can do this: one very easy way is to simply ask the client to "double the feeling of XXX!" So for Nate, we may say:

Nate: I am lying on the sun lounger and feeling the sun on my skin.

Coach: And as you are lying there and feeling the sun on your skin, how is the rest of your body feeling now?

Nate: Really relaxed and calm.

Coach: Yes…really relaxed and calm…and I wonder what it feels like if you were to double that feeling of relaxation and calm?

Nate: Mmmmm.

Coach: Feels good, right? So go ahead and double it again…really feeling more and more deeply relaxed and completely calm.

Another way is to get in touch even more with the specific feeling in the body and begin to build this up. Every emotion we experience causes our brain to produce certain chemicals that have an effect on the physical body; our body then sends signals back to the brain letting us know our body is in the desired state. These messages sent back from the body to the brain are how we 'feel' our feelings. Getting in touch even more deeply, and engaging our unconscious minds in the process, has a powerful effect. The unconscious mind communicates with us through images, sensations, colors and metaphors. We can utilize all of these to help enhance positive resources. Let's go back to Nate lying on the sun lounger on the beach:

Nate: I am lying on the sun lounger and feeling the sun on my skin.

Coach: And as you are lying there and feeling the sun on your skin, how is the rest of your body feeling now?

Nate: Really relaxed and calm.

Coach: That's right, you are feeling really relaxed and calm, and where in your body are you feeling relaxed and calm?

Nate: In my shoulders.

Coach: Right …in your shoulders, and when you are feeling so very relaxed in your shoulders, what color is that relaxed and calm feeling for you now?

Nate: Hmmm…it is a beautiful blue, just like the ocean.

Coach: A beautiful blue just like the ocean, in your shoulders… and I wonder when that beautiful blue like the ocean is going to spread to the rest of your body and feel soooo good there too?

Nate: Mmmm it already has.

Coach: And what is the temperature of your beautiful blue ocean?

Nate: Oh, it is lovely and warm.

Coach: Is there any sound?

Nate: Just a gentle hum.

We take in and experience everything through a combination of our 5 senses. In NLP these are known as our 'Representational Systems' because once the information is experienced, we represent it internally in only one of these categories: Visual, Auditory, Kinesthetic, Gustatory and Olfactory. Each one of these modalities has further distinctions or submodalities. For example, if we take the Visual Modality, we can further define the an experience by considering if the picture we make in our mind's eye is in color or black and white, is it moving or still, what size is the picture, etc. These finer distinctions are known as submodalities and we can use these to help build a wonderfully strong resource. We used some of them in the above example: color, temperature, sounds. We can also use submodalities to enhance a scene before asking the client to associate into it.

Coach: So when was the last time and place you were feeling really calm?

Nate: About 6 months ago.

Coach: Where were you?

Nate: On the beach in Puerto Rico.

Coach: Lovely…I want you to make a picture of yourself on the beach in Puerto Rico…what were you doing?

Nate: I was lying on the sun lounger.

Coach: So now, make a picture of yourself lying on that sun lounger…what were you hearing?

Nate: I could hear the ocean gently coming onto the shore and kids playing and having fun.

Coach: So now let's make this picture bigger and brighter…bring it a bit closer, and as you do I want to notice how you are feeling…

Nate: Oh yeah…I want to get on that lounger again!

Coach: Ok…go ahead…step into the 'you' in the picture, fully and completely, seeing the beach, hearing the sound of the ocean and feeling really calm.

Nate: (taking a big breath and letting it out slowly)…Mmmmmmmmmm.

Coach: That's right, it feels really good to be so completely relaxed, doesn't it?

How do we know if they are Associated into the Resource State?

Once again, to determine if and when the client is associating into the Resource State, we are calibrating exactly how our client is now behaving; in particular we are looking and listening for the unconscious clues that they are giving us, the voice tone, pauses, tempo, their physical stance, gestures, facial expression, skin color and so on.

Sometimes a client may be saying that they are feeling relaxed, and yet you observe that they are twiddling their fingers. Their unconscious mind is letting you know that they are not fully and completely aligned with the is feeling of relaxation, and they you may need to do some more work to help them really associate into the feeling. We are looking for congruency in the words they are saying, and how their entire physiognomy is responding too. This means the conscious mind (the words they are saying) and their unconscious mind (everything else about how they are saying it and how the body is reacting) are completely aligned.

Another possibility is when you see your clients going to a resourceful state, but it doesn't appear to be very powerful. In this case, the most obvious solution is simply to increase the size of the Resource State using some of the techniques described above. As Richard Bandler, the co-founder of NLP, says: If you need a magnifying glass to see the Resource State, then it's too small. The second thing to realize is that the Meta Pattern is an iterative process; we can run the same loop again and again and again, and each time it reduces the problem, and increases the resource, a little more. So even a seemingly small state can ultimately make a big difference if the pattern is looped several times.

The following is an example from a regression using the HNLP regression technique.

Coach: So what resource do you have now, that if the younger you had that resource the situation would have been different?

Client: I don't know. There's nothing...

Coach: You said you were very organized at work...

Client: Yes I am.

Coach: If that younger you had been able to organize her experiences, how would it have been different for her?

Client: I guess she would've had more idea as to what was going on...

Coach: That's right. Now I want you to float into that younger you, and notice how that's different now. And allow the years to pass so that younger you begins to grow up... Until she becomes you, here, now...

Client: It's a little different.

Coach: That's right, and because it's different, you're also different now, you learned something from this experience, and you're not the same person you were even five minutes ago. So based on these new learnings, what do you know now but you didn't know then? And send those learnings back to that you down there, and notice how it's different.

Client: Yes, I seem to have more choices now...

Coach: That's right. You have more choices. And when you're ready, you can float into that younger you and feel what it's like to have more choices, now, allowing the years to pass, feel yourself growing up… Until you become the you in this room here and now.

Client: That feels much different.

Coach: That's right. Because it feels much different that means that you've learned even more as a result of this experience. So what resources do you have right now, that you didn't have then, that if the younger you had those everything would be different?

Starting off with even the smallest amount of the resource can create massive change if the pattern is repeated on an iterative basis, looping into the experience again and again each time with a slightly greater resource.

What do we do if we can't Associate them into the Resource State?

Occasionally a client might find it difficult to associate into a resource. If this is the case, then a couple of things might be happening. Firstly, they may not have fully dissociated from the Problem State, and so we're still on step two of the Meta Pattern.

When we do the dissociation from the problem or Present State, it is important that we fully move the attention away from the problem to something that is entirely separate from the issue. This is why we sometimes ask a question that is completely unrelated for example, "Those shoes look really comfortable, where did you get them?" This creates a moment of confusion in the client's mind while they are directed towards something new. This shakes them out of the looping pattern of the problem. If your client is having a hard time finding a resource, make sure that they are fully dissociated from the issue!

The second possibility is that the client is not used to feeling resourceful. In this case, again, even a small resourceful state may be sufficient as long as the pattern is looped a number of times. See the example above.

Another consideration if a client is having a hard time finding a resource is that there is actually something else going on; maybe the problem they have stated is not really the problem! Sometimes a client may come in and state their issue, yet omit an aspect of it that we need to address first. This is sometimes the case when the client has a belief about their ability to change. The client may say something like, "I want to quit smoking," and we could go through all the steps of finding the last time and place they smoked, etc. yet somehow they find it hard to feel how they want to be. If they have a belief like "I can't change," "This won't work," "I'm never going to succeed" that is there but has been unvoiced, then this belief is probably interfering with the process and would need to be addressed first. Going through the steps of any change pattern with a nagging voice of "This won't work" is always going to prove tricky and the overarching belief is what needs to be altered before any other changes can take place.

Finally, some clients simply suffer from low self-esteem. Not only do they find it difficult to associate into a resourceful state, but also they may believe that it's impossible for them to do so. In this case it may be more important to work on self-esteem before we move on to the presenting problem.

Chapter Eight:

Step 4: The Collapse

What is a Collapse?

So now we have moved our client's attention and emotions through 3 steps of the Meta Pattern; we have associated them into the problem, dissociated from the problem, and have built up a wonderful associated resource experience for them. It is time to take the resource to the Problem State. This is known as 'the Collapse.'

A collapse is basically firing off the two states (problem and resource) at exactly the same time. Neurologically, we are lighting up two very different networks simultaneously. By doing this we are creating a new neurological pathway, linking together two areas that had previously never been linked. Now, what is most important is for the resource state to be more powerful than the Problem State, in order for it to 'collapse' that part. This is Hebbs Law at work AND the beginning of the Neural Pruning we mentioned before. We are creating a new neurological pathway from whatever set the client off into a negative feeling or behavior to a new, more positive feeling and behavior. At the same time, because that old pathway is not being used, it begins to become 'overgrown'; the neurons become less sensitive and do not fire so easily and eventually become unusable.

The more we repeat this cycle, looping this pattern, building the resource up each time, the stronger we are building the new pathway. So now the situation or trigger that once led the client to feeling bad leads them to feeling good. The old pathway that leads from whatever triggered them into feeling bad is now the very thing that will set them off on their new pathway toward feeling resourceful.

How do we do a Collapse?

The collapse is very simple; as soon as the client is in a big Resource State, we ask them to look back at the problem trigger thus firing the two states at the same time.

So let's think back to the example of Nate. Nate got nervous when he had to make his weekly presentation to his colleagues and he wants to feel calm. We have seen Nate 'doing' his problem, have dissociated him from the problem, and have associated him into feeling really calm, building up the Resource State so Nate is feeling amazingly calm and relaxed. Now we will see how we do the collapse with Nate:

Coach: OK…go ahead…step into the 'you' in the picture, fully and completely, seeing the beach, hearing the sound of the ocean and feeling really calm.

Nate: (taking a big breath and letting it out slowly)…Mmmmmmmmm.

Coach: That's right, it feels really good to be so completely relaxed, doesn't it? And as you are feeling so wonderfully calm, I want you to think back to last Monday in the conference room, hearing your boss's voice and notice how it is different now…

Nate: Oh, that feels much different, so much calmer.

How do we know if there has been a Collapse?

We will know if there has been a collapse simply by calibrating to how the client reacts and responds to what was their problem. With Nate, the problem had changed and he felt much calmer when revisiting the specific event. Even if the problem hasn't entirely collapsed, nevertheless it will be different, and we are asking the client to specifically "Notice how it is different now." We are intentionally asking them to search for and focus on how things have already changed.

From this moment, we don't refer to "the problem" any more, just the few words to jog the memory about "the conference room" or a vague reference to "the way you used to feel." The reason we do this is because the problem will have changed, in a big way, or a small way, or any way in-between and so we are focusing on the positive changes and not revivifying the issue or problem.

What do we do if there is no Collapse?

The Meta Pattern is not only a structure of change work; it is also an incredibly useful guide for us to know exactly where the client is in the process of change. If the collapse doesn't appear to be working, then a few things may be going on. Firstly, we would want to check in with the client as to what they are experiencing 'now.' Remember, your client may have had this issue or problem for years and years and have become so used to feeling a certain way that is it more difficult for them to begin to look for how they have indeed changed.

Some people sort for things that are the same and some people sort for things that are different. We even run internal unconscious program for the way we 'sort' our experiences.

Here's a fun way to experience this:

Find two coins, maybe a nickel and a quarter, and ask someone, "What is the relationship between these two coins?" See if they naturally tell you about the things that are different between the coins, or if they naturally tell you about the things that are similar.

The client might just be running a 'same' program, so when they are asked to check in with themselves about how they used to feel, it is easier for them to find all the ways they are feeling 'the same' about it. This is one possibility.

Another reason that the client may be unable to do a collapse is because the Resource State is not powerful enough. The Resource State, the good feelings, has to be larger than the initial problem. This is why we will spend sufficient time building up the Resource State, for example by asking the client to find a color or a movement for that positive feeling and spinning, increasing, and doubling this feeling. As soon as we see the client move into a positive feeling, we use it. We help them to increase the feeling and then take it back mentally to the event for the collapse.

The client may also have difficulty with the collapse if they have not been very specific with the event. If you think back to how we associated them into the Problem State, we helped the client to go back to a certain time, a very specific moment, just one event in particular. We asked them about the time and the place, what time of day, where they are, what they are seeing, hearing and feeling. If you have not moved the client into a particular moment and have instead allowed them to be a bit more vague, like, "It happened a couple of times over the past few weeks," then they have not 'lit up' the precise neural networks inside their mind and therefore the resource is not being attached in the correct place; hence the collapse is incomplete or doesn't happen at all.

Remember Hebbs Law: "Neurons that fire together, wire together." We are effectively creating a new neural pathway, a new way for these neurons to fire together and so we have to be sure that we have the precise starting point for the new path!

Chapter Nine:

The Meta Pattern and the Classic Patterns of NLP

In this next chapter we will be looking at how some of the classic NLP patterns fit into the structure of The Meta Pattern. If you are familiar with the NLP patterns, then this will be of great interest to you. If you are new to NLP, you may wish to familiarize yourself with these patterns, or just skip ahead. Either way is better.

The 'art' of NLP is having the ability to 'dance' with the client. Now, I don't mean we get up and salsa during the session; what I mean is having the skill to expertly calibrate your client, being able to figure out how the client is doing their problem and calibrate to how they are changing throughout a session.

Coupled with this is having the flexibility and knowledge to move in any direction at any time during a session, and to elegantly flow one piece of an NLP pattern (or other change modality) into another. It is fairly rare in my practice that I will go though an entire NLP pattern with a client in the 'step-by-step ' manner in which I was taught it. Having the knowledge of the Meta Pattern structure enables you to know exactly where the client is at any moment and to spend more time or less time focusing on one area or spend time enhancing or decreasing states. It provides the structure of the cycle of change so that you can calibrate exactly to where your client is at any moment and know how, when and where to begin to lead them toward their desired change.

We can think of the NLP patterns as 'training wheels' or essential building blocks of NLP change work. Once you are familiar with the steps, you can add in the Meta Pattern structure to further enhance your knowledge and understanding of how each of the steps function, and the reason why you are doing them. With this knowledge you can begin to 'dance' with your client, following the Meta Pattern structure, calibrating to your client's changes, using your experience and intuition to guide you into leading your client towards change.

But before we get there, let's take a step back and take a look at a few of the well-known NLP patterns and how they fit into the Meta Pattern.

Let me take you back to when I had recently completed my NLP Practitioner class, and, with a dozen or so patterns and lists buzzing around in my head, was sitting in class in Atlanta with John Overdurf, coming to grips with the Meta Pattern. I was so excited because it made everything click into place for me. I could see how this gave me the structure of all change work, a structure for a session, and I could also look at each NLP pattern and notice how they fit into the structure too.

I hope that you are equally excited about the Meta Pattern and are beginning to think of how each of the classical NLP patterns aligns with it. Being curious about such things is excellent, and I encourage you to go through the NLP patterns yourself. I will also give you some help by going through a few of the classic NLP patterns that you will find in an NLP Practitioner course. I will just be giving a brief step-by-step procedure of the patterns. Please refer to other books in this series for further details and greater explanation of these patterns.

The Meta Pattern and The Circle of Excellence

The Circle of Excellence is a lovely pattern, one of my personal favorites and one that I frequently use with clients. On the surface it is pretty simple: ask your client to stand up, imagine a circle on the floor in front of them, fill the circle with amazing resources, and finally step into the circle, into those resources. Once the client has experienced stepping into the Circle of Excellence, you might invite them to take the circle with them so they will have it when they need it.

Most clients, even clients who are not very emotionally demonstrative, will feel wonderful after the Circle of Excellence.

Here is the pattern and how it fits into the Meta Pattern:

1. Discuss what the issue/problem is where they want to feel differently (Associate into the Problem State)
2. Imagine a circle on the floor. Decide what resource you would like to place in the circle (Dissociate from the Problem State)
3. Step into the circle to fully experience the resources (Associate into the Resource State)
4. Think back to the issue and notice how it is different with your "Circle of Excellence" (Collapse)

The Circle of Excellence clearly and neatly fits into the structure of the Meta Pattern. If this were the whole story, perhaps the Meta Pattern would be simply an interesting observation on the nature of change. But it is much more than this; when doing a pattern, even one as simple as the Circle of Excellence, the Meta Pattern allows you as a coach to become much more powerful, effective, and elegant in doing your work.

In order to demonstrate this, let's consider some of the things that can go wrong when doing the Circle of Excellence:

Failing to attach the change to the context of the problem

Sometimes a coach will do a wonderful Circle of Excellence, but not attach the resources to the context of the problem. The interaction might go something like this:

Coach: What do you want to work through today?

Client: I want to feel more confident...

Coach: Great, let's do this exercise called the Circle of Excellence... Imagine a circle in front of you, see yourself in the circle feeling totally confident, and step into the circle, feel how good that feels...

Client: That feels amazing!

Coach: Great! That will be $100 please!

Obviously we are exaggerating here, but we certainly see situations where a coach leads the client to feel amazing in the session, but it doesn't translate to feeling great in the outside world where they actually need it. The way to translate a pattern like the Circle of Excellence into a real-world change is to make sure that, as a coach, you first associate your clients into the context of the problem (associate into the problem), and that finally, after creating a state of confidence in the client, get them to reassociate into the context of the problem, this time experiencing that context from that state of confidence (the collapse). The coach then needs to repeat this process a number of times until the confidence becomes wired to the context that was previously problematic.

Failing to associate the client into a resource, or into a sufficiently powerful resource

We have, unfortunately, seen coaches demonstrate the Circle off Excellence without paying attention to whether or not the client is actually associating into the Resource State. It's not enough to simply have them step into an imaginary circle; that circle has to be full of resourceful energy!

There are two main mistakes that coaches sometimes make. The first mistake is failing to 'lead' the client into the resource. I remember seeing a coach demonstrate the Circle of Excellence...

Coach [leaning casually against the wall with his arms folded]: See yourself in the circle looking confident [sounding bored]... And when you're ready, step into that and notice how you feel...

Client [looking like she did when she was in the Problem State]: Uh, ok, I guess I feel better...

Coach [still sounding bored]: Great, double that feeling.

The 'trick' with the Circle of Excellence, if there is one, is to do everything you need to do as a coach so that you see the client becoming resourceful BEFORE they step into the circle! Something like this:

Coach [speaking confidently]: See yourself in the circle feeling totally confident... Notice how you're standing [the coach shifts her posture, straightening...the client also straightens] there when you're feeling confident...[coach begins to get excited]... Notice how you're breathing... The expression on your face...[client continues to look more and more confident...]... Now step into the circle and notice how you feel...

In the above example, the coach does not let the client to step into the circle until the coach is absolutely certain that the client is feeling confident. The coach then invites the client to "Step into the circle and notice how you feel…" The client will follow the instructions in the order given; she will first step into the circle, and then she will put her attention on how she feels, which of course is a sense of confidence. The client comes to believe that by stepping into the circle, she has become confident, whereas in fact she became confident before she stepped into the circle. In the client's mind, the Circle of Excellence becomes the cause of her confidence!

The coach will also loop through stepping into the circle with the resource, then stepping out of the circle to add another resource, then stepping back into the circle to experience that feeling. Each time the coach asks the client to step out of the circle and find another resource, the coach is helping the client to build up the resource so it is even more powerful. Only when you as the coach, looking at your client, consider that the resource is very powerful will you ask them to "Look at that whole situation and notice how it's different now!" This step can also be looped a number of times to firmly attach the resource to the context that was previously problematic.

After the collapse, when the client has built up their circle sufficiently and attached it to the context of the problem, they are ready to 'take the circle with them." At this point I encourage the client to be creative and follow his or her own inner guidance in respect to the method of 'taking the circle.' Some popular choices have been to pick the circle up and put it in their pocket, or wrap it around themselves like a cape. I have had a few clients who have decided to eat their circle, or even to inhale it. Whichever way the client chooses to bring the resource back inside them is perfect. Once this is done, we can ask them to think back to the problem and notice how it is different now having collapsed the problem with the massive resource of their Circle of Excellence.

The Meta Pattern and The Stuck Meta Resource Pattern

This is a classic NLP pattern and follows the Meta Pattern beautifully. In fact, you can think of Stuck-Meta-Resource as the manifestation of the Meta Pattern using spatial anchors. Here are the steps over the pattern:

1. The coach asks the client to select 3 points around them, and label them "Stuck," "Meta" and "Resource." The coach will be leading the client into the Problem State, dissociating them from the Problem State, and then associating them into the Resource State as the client steps into each location.

2. The coach will invite the client to "Step into the 'Stuck' position." The coach asks the client about his problem, and about the last time and place he experienced his problem until the coach sees the client begin to associate into the Problem State. (Step 1 of the Meta Pattern – associate into the Problem State.)

3. The coach now asks the client to step out of the Stuck position, and into the Meta position. The coach will then point toward the Stuck position and begin to use dissociative language until the coach sees the client is dissociated from the problem. For example, the coach might say, "Look at that 'you', over there [pointing to the 'stuck' position]… describe what you see when you look at him, over there…" Remember to use third person terms, i.e. "the John over there"…"her shoulders look slumped…" (Step 2 of the Meta Pattern – dissociate from the Problem State.)

4. Now the coach will invite the client to "Look toward the 'Resource' position. Describe the Ideal self, how are you looking when you're feeling totally resourceful?" As in the

Circle off Excellence, the coach will 'go first' by beginning to shift into a more resourceful state; this will be reflected in the coach's physiology, gestures, tone of voice, and so on. Only when the coach sees the client begin to follow her into this resourceful state will the coach move to the next step and invite her client to:

"Step into the 'Resource' position, stepping into that new you, and notice how good that feels to take on the physiology, breathing, and beliefs of the resourceful you…" (Step 3 of the Meta Pattern – associate into the Resource State.)

5. The coach can now invite the client to, "Step back to the 'Stuck' position, this time taking all those resources with you…" The coach leads the client through the steps of the pattern, getting quicker each time (Step 4 of the Meta Pattern – the Collapse).

Each time the client is stepping from the Resource position to the Stuck position, they are doing a collapse because they are taking the resources back to the initial problem. Lighting up these two neurological networks at the same time will cause something new to happen, because we are beginning to link the two and create a new neurological network. It is important in every pattern to ensure that the client in fully associated into the resource and to build it up to be a very powerful feeling so as to collapse the negative state.

The Visual Squash

The Visual Squash is a wonderful and versatile NLP pattern. It is usually used to deal with, and integrate, two 'parts' of a client where those two parts are in disagreement about a choice or behavior.

For a complete description of the Visual Squash, you can read *The Visual Squash*, a part of our NLP Mastery Series, which describes the pattern in great detail. For now, let's just assume that the client has a decision to make: they have been offered a new position which may provide them with a great opportunity for personal growth, but to do so they will have to leave the security of the well-paying job they now hold.

In terms of classical NLP, a problem of this type is called an 'exclusive or,' meaning the client has decided they can have one thing, or the other, but not both. Of course, on a more cognitive and logical basis the client could simply list the pros and cons of each option and make a decision accordingly.

The problem with this sort of cognitive approach is that the client is likely to feel they have missed out on something no matter which option they choose. Leading the client through a 'parts-integration' allows them to move forward being completely happy with their choice, and it may even allow them to identify a third option which combines the best of both.

These steps off the Visual Squash are as follows:

1. Discuss the conflict. (Associate into the Problem State)

2. Put each part onto the palms of the hands and create a symbol for each. This is another point where the power of the Meta Pattern becomes apparent; listening to the client speak, it may sound as if his problem is that he can't make up his mind. If this were indeed the case, then the cognitive approach of listing the pros and cons would be appropriate, and if you are purely a business coach, this might be a great technique to use.

However, if you are coaching on a more holistic basis, and in particular if you know the client has already considered the pros and cons in depth and still faces the inner conflict, then something else is going on. The problem is not that the client can't make up his mind, but rather that any decision results in inner conflict.

Therefore, in order to dissociate from the problem, we need to remove the conflicting parts from inside the client, and most especially to separate them so they are no longer in direct conflict. I remember as a child riding in the backseat of our parents' car with my brother, and my parents placing a cushion in between us to prevent us from fighting! Taking the two conflicting parts of the client and placing one on each hand has a similar effect! (Dissociate from the Problem State)

3. The coach will now invite the client to 'chunk-up' on each part by asking, "What positive things is this doing for you? What is its positive intention?" The coach continues to ask for higher and higher, and more and more abstract, positive intentions until a shared positive intention is found. This shared positive intention, one that is common to both the conflicting parts, provides a path through which the parts can begin to interact in a more positive way.

The coach will now begin to build a new 'part' that incorporates the best of both of the previously conflicting parts. For example, she might ask, "What can this part learn from that part? What can this part teach to that part?" The coach is listening for the client to begin to describe the two, or now three, parts seamlessly, using the same positive attributes for each.

This new, combined part, which has access to the resources of both conflicting parts, becomes the new resource. (Associate into the Resource State)

4. The Visual Squash is a very hypnotic pattern. The above steps will normally be combined with hypnotic catalepsy during which the client's hands will unconsciously come together. This begins the process of 'collapse.' A new symbol is also likely to appear representing the new integrated part, further stabilizing the collapse.

Finally, the coach will invite the client, consciously or unconsciously, to "Bring the new symbol into your heart or mind or body in whatever way makes sense to you..." This may be done simply by encouraging the client's cataleptic hands to move towards their body. This completes the collapse by bringing the new integrated part inside, where previously the two conflicting parts were fighting!

V-K Dissociation (the Fast Phobia Fix)

V-K Dissociation, sometimes called the Fast Phobia Fix, is a technique intended to reduce an unconscious negative reaction to a stimulus. For example, the basis of a phobia is that the sufferer sees the phobic stimulus and has the phobic response without needing to think about it on a conscious level. For example, if someone has a phobia of penguins and they see a penguin, they don't need to stop and think, "A penguin, I'm afraid of those – I better be afraid now!" Instead, as soon as they see the penguin, they immediately and automatically experience their fear.

Responses such as this are caused by a brain process called the 'amygdala hijack.' During the amygdala hijack, the stimulus (the sight of the penguin) is processed by the amygdala before it even gets to the visual cortex at the back of the brain, and way before it is routed to the higher brain areas in the prefrontal cortex (PFC). By the time the stimulus is analyzed on the level of the PFC (whether or not there is a real threat), the sufferer's neurology and physiology has already entered panic-mode!

V-K Dissociation allows the trigger to be seen or imagined, while the amygdala is kept in a playful sense of ease. This retrains the amygdala to no longer react with the panic response as it did previously.

1. Discuss the trigger for problem or issue. (Step 1 of the Meta Pattern – associate into the Problem State)

Please note that you do not need to associate your client into a phobic response! Indeed, if you do so you may spend much of the rest of the coaching session calming them down! Most often if somebody comes to see you so you can help them with a phobia or similar issue, you will see them begin to associate into the negative state as soon as they tell you what they are phobic to.

2. Because a phobia or similar reaction to an external stimulus is so strong, the key step, and the backbone of the V-K Dissociation pattern, is dissociating them from the reaction and keeping them dissociated. There are several ways of doing this: in the classical V-K Dissociation you, as the coach, might ask the client to "Imagine yourself in an old movie theatre. There is a small blank screen in the distance. Now, imagine floating out of your self and into the projection booth. From the projection booth you can control the movie, and you can look down at yourself watching the movie on that screen way over there…"

This technique of 'watching your self watching yourself' is called a double-dissociation. It is intended to make it much more difficult for the client to reassociate into the problem. There are several other ways for achieving this as well, such as watching the movie on the screen of a tiny iPhone; this makes it virtually impossible for the client to imagine floating into that movie.

Whichever technique is used, you can say to your client something like, "On the screen, place a still image in black and white of the scene preceding the event, when you are completely safe... Now create a still image of the scene after the event when you are completely safe…" . These two scenes serve as the 'bookends' for the movie that will be played, keeping it confined within a safe-to-safe space. (Step 2 of the Meta Pattern – dissociate from the Problem State)

3. Ask the client to watch the movie (from safe scene to safe scene) with various submodality shifts, often incorporating humor, and always giving them control. For example, you might ask them to run the movie very fast, backward, in black and white, perhaps adding funny, quirky things such as circus music. If appropriate, you can ask the client to float into the end of the movie and experience it going backwards with the fun elements. (Step 3 of the Meta Pattern – associate into the Resource State)

The important thing is that they begin to experience the trigger while staying calm or even laughing. This re-trains the amygdala to react in a different way.

4. If appropriate, you can ask the client to float into the movie and experience it going forward. Alternatively, you can ask them to think of the memory and ask them how it's different. If the presenting issue is something like a fear, you can send them to a real place where the trigger is present (perhaps the penguin house at the zoo!) to test their response. (Step 4 of the Meta Pattern – the collapse)

V-K Dissociation is a highly effective pattern for changing the experience of a traumatic event. It uses a double dissociation (the movie screen, then the watching of watching the movie) in order to stop the client from associating into the problem. We only need to associate the client into the problem at beginning this pattern just enough for the correct neurological network to be lit up and to know exactly where to attach the new resource, something they'll likely to do as soon as they tell you what the problem is!

I have found that many clients who have traumatic events in their pasts will associate very quickly or will come into the office already associated, so the trick is to use this double dissociation to keep them out of the problem while changing it. Now that you understand the Meta Pattern, you will see that the key to the V-K Dissociation is step two of the Meta Pattern, the dissociation. This insight allows you to use the tools of the V-K Dissociation pattern to create powerful dissociation whenever it is needed. For example, if you are doing any other NLP pattern, you can use the idea of the movie screen dissociation, the iPhone dissociation, or even the double dissociation, where you are otherwise having trouble dissociating the client from the problem.

The Swish

The Swish is one of the most powerful and generative of the classical NLP patterns. It is most often used for habits and compulsions such as nail-biting or smoking, although in fact it can be used to create powerful generative states that allow the client to achieve amazing goals.

For an in-depth discussion of the Swish and its full potential, read our book *The Swish* in the NLP Mastery series. For this example, we will simply assume that the client bites his nails, and wants to stop.

As always, the first thing to do is to associate the client into the context of the problem. In the case of the Swish, we need to get extremely specific as to this context, asking them precisely what they see immediately before they engage in the nail-biting, the 'trigger picture.' (Step 1 of the Meta Pattern- associate into the Problem State)

The next step of course is to disassociate the client. In the case of the Swish, used to change habits such as nail-biting, this is generally relatively easy because there is usually not a strong negative state associated with the behavior. The client may feel annoyed that they bite their nails, but they are unlikely to feel fear or even terrified like in the V-K Dissociation. So to dissociate the clients, you can generally just say something like, "Now, blank the screen…" (Step 2 of the Meta Pattern-dissociate from the Problem State)

Our students often find it difficult to immediately fit the Swish in the context of the Meta Pattern. You see, in the Swish we are going to ask our client to make a picture of themselves as they want to be (the 'outcome picture'): "I want you to make an image of how you would like to be instead…" Later we will then exchange the trigger picture with this new outcome picture. The reason it seems more difficult to fit the Swish into the structure of the Meta Pattern is that the outcome picture remains dissociated (note that in some versions of the Swish we do associate the client into the outcome picture, but in the classic Swish we do not do this). Once again, this is because we need to properly identify the resource the coach is seeking to install in the client. The resource is not 'being this new you'; in fact, behavioral research suggests that associating into an outcome actually reduces the motivation to work towards that outcome. It is as if the unconscious mind, once associated into the outcome, already has the benefits and therefore is not prepared to make the effort. The resource the coach is actually trying to install is desire: the client's desire to become the new person they want to become. This desire is created by seeing the outcome, the 'new you,' as almost but not quite within arm's reach. (Step 3 of the Meta Pattern – associate into the Resource State – desire)

Once the client has that outcome picture, the 'new you,' it is time to do the Swish. The Swish is actually a tool that allows you to quickly and easily do a visual collapse. The coach will ask the client to "Shrink the outcome image, the new you, down to the size of a postage stamp and place it in the trigger picture. Now, as you see the trigger picture with the 'new you' embedded in it, shoot it way out into the distance…the image will quickly come close again, but this time it will be the picture of the 'new you'... (Step 4 of the Meta Pattern – the collapse)

The coach will then ask the client to blank the screen and repeat the above steps to condition the change.

Once again, the Meta Pattern can provide wonderful insights into the Swish. With the Meta Pattern in mind, we can see that the Swish is in fact a way of collapsing the resource and Problem States using the visual sense. Once you understand this, you can begin to incorporate the Swish into all your change work as a rapid collapse. (Step 4 of the Meta Pattern)

The Six-Step Reframe

The Six-Step Reframe is a wonderful pattern from classical NLP to quickly and elegantly change an unwanted behavior or feeling. In our opinion, the Six-Step Reframe is in fact a massive gratitude-trance in which the change takes place. The gratitude-trance is created by a process of fractionation (opening and closing the eyes), while repeatedly thanking the unconscious mind for everything it is doing for us. This, more than anything else (in our opinion), is a resource that the coach leads the client to access during the Six-Step Reframe.

Here are the steps of the Six-Step Reframe:

1. Discuss the issue or problem. (Step 1 of the Meta Pattern - associate into the Problem State)

2. Establish communication with the unconscious mind. Ask the unconscious mind to give "yes" and "no" signals. Very often these signals are specific feelings or sensations in the body.

Turning the problem behavior or emotion into a somatic sensation or feeling in the body dissociates the clients from the problem because these somatic feelings become 'signals' as opposed to negative emotions. (Step 2 of the Meta Pattern- dissociate from the Problem State)

As you, the coach, lead your client through the remaining steps of the Six-Step Reframe, you are going to be repeatedly asking the client to "Go inside ..." and then to "...thank your unconscious." This creates fractionation, and a feeling of gratitude toward the unconscious: a 'gratitude-trance.' It is this gratitude-trance that allows new ways of acting and being to develop within the client.

3. "Go inside and ask your unconscious mind if it knows the positive intention of the behavior... Go inside and thank your unconscious..."

4. "Go inside and ask the unconscious to generate 20 or more alternative behaviors... Go inside and thank your unconscious..." (step 3 of the Meta Pattern)

Finally, we bring the newly selected behavioral feeling back to the context of the problem...

5. "Go inside and ask your unconscious to select one of the behaviors and commit to trying it on for a period of 2 weeks, and if it is working, to continue the new positive behavior." (Step 4 of the Meta Pattern - the collapse)

6. Ecology check – ask if all aspects are completely aligned with this new behavior.

The Six Step Reframe is a very unconscious pattern, and the hypnotic aspect can be deepened in a delightful manner. I tend to break down each step into a series of smaller steps and ask my clients to let me know when they have completed each one. Then I ask them to "Go back inside and thank your unconscious mind." By doing this I am utilizing the hypnotic phenomena of fractionation, bringing my client gently in and out of trance, knowing that each time they go back inside that are able to go deeper. They are able to associate into the Resource State on a very deep unconscious level. Many times my clients will come back and say something like, "I don't know what new resources were generated, but I know that they were." This change work has taken place on a very deep unconscious level.

Chapter Ten:

The Conversational Meta Pattern: "The Coaching Pattern"

Up until now, we have been focusing on the Meta Pattern as a structure: how it underpins all change work patterns and gives us a clear and succinct route to follow when working with clients. We have been viewing the Meta Pattern as a process rather than a technique or pattern in and of itself.

Most of the standard patterns in NLP consist of a number of steps to be followed in order to get the change. These steps may include physical movement, for example, when using the Circle of Excellence we ask the client to stand up, imagine a circle on the floor, and move in and out of the circle to access positive resources. In the Stuck Meta Resource pattern, we ask the client to move between three different areas of the room. With the Visual Squash, we ask the client to hold out their hands in front of them.

For many clients, especially in a therapeutic context, asking them to move around or to hold out their hands is fine. However, for some people these requests may seem a little strange, particularly if you are working in a more formal business context and you may sense a hesitancy to follow along with your suggestions.

Fortunately there is a conversational version of the Meta Pattern that is immensely useful in these contexts. In fact, this is how I begin each and every coaching session. In a few simple sentences I am able to gather a tremendous amount of information both from the client's verbal and unconscious responses. And this is all done totally conversationally, in a very easy manner, sometimes without the clients fully realizing that we have already begun to make powerful changes for them.

Each question is designed to move the client through the four steps of the Meta Pattern. We are well aware as hypnotists and change workers that the unconscious mind is really the one we want to communicate with. The unconscious mind is where the problem exists, even though the client has become consciously aware that there is a problem, and it is also the place where we'll find the resources and the solution. So it is essential that we are aware that we need to communicate not only with the client's conscious mind, but with the unconscious mind too.

The pattern we are about to explain is called the Coaching Pattern. It is a beautiful example of multi-layered communication. This means that the coach needs to speak to the client's conscious and unconscious mind to make the change. The words that the coach uses and the questions the coach asks may be more concerned with the client's conscious mind, but the selection of the words speak to the unconscious. In addition, unconscious communication comes from the coach's tone of voice, body language and gestures, and facial expressions. All of these are vital ingredients in a piece of change work and we will see how to specifically use them to help the client to change within this particular pattern.

The Coaching Pattern Questions

There are a few standard questions that we ask when doing the Coaching Pattern. We will outline them here briefly and then discuss each one, why we use the specific language, how to deliver the question to the conscious and unconscious mind, and how they fit into the Meta Pattern.

What do you want to work through?

Tell me about a specific time and place this this happened.

What are you seeing, hearing and feeling?

That's how you've been…how do you want to be different?

And as you are feeling this…think back to that old thing and notice how it is different now!

These are the basic questions and we may ask them in a variety of different ways. We usually cycle through the Coaching Pattern a number of times throughout a session or interaction and of course will be using the client's own wording and experiences also.

So let's begin to break down the questions and take a deeper look into what we are doing and how we are doing it.

We begin by asking client, "What do you want to work through?" This appears to be a very traditional type of question that anyone would ask at the beginning of the session. It is important for you as a coach to know exactly what issue or problem the client is coming in with. The question is worded in a very specific way; we're not asking the client what the problem is, or what they want to work *on*, or to tell us about the problem. We specifically ask them what they would like to work *through*. By including this specific word, we are already giving an instruction to the unconscious mind that we are working through this problem until then end as opposed to working on and on and on!

Try it on for yourself for a moment. Think of a small issue then ask yourself how it feels to be working *on* this problem. Now ask yourself how it feels to be working *through* this problem. It has a different feel; many people report a specific kinesthetic response. There is much more movement when you consider working *through* something. So this single word is already beginning to have a positive impact on the unconscious level for your client.

Now, your client is very likely to be totally unaware that they are already beginning to change. Their mind is likely to be focusing on the issue or problem and they will begin to tell you about the problem. We are not yet at the first step of the Meta Pattern, although we are very close. We need the client to *associate* into the problem. Some clients will begin to associate into a specific time and place as soon as you ask them "What would you like to work through?" You will recognize this because you will see a change in the client's demeanor, facial expression, skin tone, and so on, and you may hear them begin to talk about the issue in the present tense.

However, oftentimes the client will begin to talk about the problem in a more general way without associating into it. If this happens, then we need to focus the client's attention to one particular time so that we can help them to associate into the event, thereby lighting up the specific neurological network associated with the problem. We do this by asking the client to "Tell me about a specific time and place that this happened." We need the event to be as specific as possible. This is an essential step in the coaching pattern as it gives us the precise place where we will attach the resource later on. Once the client has given you a specific time and place that this happened, we need to associate them into the event. We do this by asking questions such as, "Where are you? What are you seeing, hearing, and feeling?" Notice that we have changed our languaging to the present tense, thereby unconsciously leading the client into fully associating to the specific time. We need to be aware of the client's language also. If they switch to using the present tense, then they are associating and all is good. However, if they are still using the past tense and talking 'about' the problem, then we need to keep focusing them on fully experiencing this moment again. One way to do this is to repeat their answers back to them but in the present tense. So if your client says, "I saw my boss," then you could repeat, "Okay so you are seeing your boss." Sometimes your client needs a little more specific direction and you can ask them to go back to the specific time fully and completely as though they were living it now. This often helps your clients to understand exactly what you are asking him/her to do.

This is the key to change work. We are looking for the client to go back to one specific time and place and begin to feel what they are feeling. We are looking for that tiny instant when the client changes from being perfectly okay to suddenly feeling bad or unresourceful. We are searching for the key moment known as the synesthesia. This is the tipping point and it is often something that the client sees, hears, or touches in the outside world that can spark a negative thought or feeling. It is well worth taking an s much time as necessary to find the synesthesia because this gives us the exact location, the precise moment, the specific trigger point where we will need to place the resource when we collapse the problem.

Finding the synesthesia

When a client comes in to see us, they are sometimes very aware of the thing that 'sets them off,' of the thing that just makes them feel unresourceful or in a negative state. These are the clients who will say something like, "The moment I hear the tone of her voice…" or, "It happens at the split second that

I see his brow begin to furrow…" However, it is pretty rare for a client to be so very specific right off the bat. Most clients have a vague idea of what it is that sets them off or at least the context or situation that they are having difficulties with. These clients are likely to say, "It happens whenever I see my boss." Others will only have a situation or context and will say something like, "It happens at work."

You need to find the exact moment when the client's state moves from being OK/fine to feeling negative. You need to associate them into the specific context as described above and then very slowly walk them through the situation whilst in the associated state until you notice the point where there is a shift or change in their demeanor. You are looking for a split of a second in real time when something changes. You can help to hold them in this specific time and place in an associated way by asking, "What are you seeing, hearing and feeling?" Notice again the language has shifted to the present tense to help them become or remain associated. You will also be asking for and guiding their attention toward sensory information; what it is specifically that they are becoming more aware of whilst walking through this moment in search of the synesthesia.

By holding them in this space, keeping them associated, walking through every aspect slowly, you can find the synesthesia. You, as the change worker, will be looking for a shift or change in the client; this could be as big as a shudder, an exclamation or a sigh, or as subtle as a fleeting look across the face, a slight change in lip movement or eye movement, or a subtle shift in breathing. It is important that you calibrate your client constantly, observing all changes and being ready to ask, "Oh, what was that?" or, "What's happening now?" The client's body and/or breathing will tell you first, so it is important to become exquisitely skilled at observing changes and to always be ready to ask your client what is happening.

Once you have noticed this sort of shift or change, you have likely found the synesthesia. At this moment, you will want to backtrack slightly through the experience and run through it again to test if they have a similar reaction at the same precise moment. This will clarify that you have the exact moment of change, the synesthesia, and that you have lit up the neurological network associated with it. This also gives you the precise moment to attach the resource later in the pattern.

You have now completed the first step of the Meta Pattern, the "associate into the Problem State." You have the precise context, the trigger or synesthesia, you have observed the client's state and noted their behavior, which allows you to know exactly where you will later attach the resource for change.

The next step is to "dissociate from the Problem State," and you will do this by utilizing what we call 'the Move.' To do this, we ask a specific worded question, whilst also gesturing to specific places. This one statement and question involves multi-layered communication, and allows you to speak to both the conscious and unconscious mind at the same time. We will break this down to explain exactly how we are doing this:

You as coach will ask, "That's how you've been... How do you want to be different?"

To the conscious mind, it is a perfectly normal question. Having talked about the problem or the issue, the client will likely be expecting some direction towards an outcome. Consciously they will be beginning to search for how they would like to be.

However, if we look more closely at the language used within this, we can begin to notice a number of things. Firstly, you are directionalizing the unconscious mind towards what they want to have, or how they want to behave. As humans, we have a tendency toward the negative, called a 'negativity bias,' and it is important for you as a coach to help the client to state their outcome in the positive. For example, a client may come with this issue of stage fright and at this moment they may say something like, "I don't want to be nervous when I make the speech." Although this sounds like they are describing what they want to have happen, it is actually stated as something that they don't want; it is expressed in the negative. The unconscious mind is very literal and it will search for exactly what is told to search for. For example, if I ask you, "Do not think of a blue elephant...whatever you do, don't think of a blue elephant!" The likelihood is that you in fact did think of a blue elephant. It is almost as though your mind says, "Right...what is it that I am not supposed to think about...let me make a picture of that so I can be certain not to think about it." And of course before you know it, you have made a picture of whatever you are trying not to think of. The same is true of "I don't want to be nervous when I make a speech." The unconscious mind makes an image of being scared as it reminds itself of what not to think about.

You have to encourage your client to state their outcome positively, directly asking them to say what they *do* want. For example, you could ask, "So if you don't want to be nervous, what DO you want?"

This statement also uses temporal languaging; once again you are speaking to the client's conscious and the unconscious mind. The first part you say is, "That's how you've BEEN..." Here we have intentionally moved the issue or problem into the past in a very elegant and subtle way, and then you will ask, "How do you want to be different?" In this short question we utilize a couple of the things: firstly the temporal language of moving toward the now/future with, "How do you want to be different?" And at the same time you are also layering in an embedded command of '...be different.' Again, subtlety moving the client's mind away from the problem and guiding them towards their outcome.

Linguistically you are already beginning to shape the change. You will also use a specific gesture to consolidate and enhance the communication with the client's unconscious mind. After all, 55% of our communication is our body language, and that includes gestures. Our unconscious mind recognizes and understands this, so the Move is an important part of the Coaching Pattern. When we make the statement "That's how you've been…" we take our right hand and sweep down and away towards the floor. It is as though we are taking the image/thought/ideas associated with the problem and literally sweeping them away.

There is also a reason we are doing this with our right hand; you see, each one of has an unconscious timeline within us. Take a moment now and just point to where your past is, the place where you keep memories and things that happened a while ago. Most people have their past on their left, or possibly behind them. By sweeping down with your right hand, you are indicating to the client's unconscious mind to place that issue into their past, i.e. toward their left. Remember, we have to be the mirror image for the client. When we as the change worker indicate with our right hand, it is pointing to the client's left hand side. We do this part of the Move as we say the words, "That's how you've been…" So now our words and gestures are all aligned with moving the problem into the client's past.

The next part of the Move is done when we ask the client, "How do you want to be different?" This time we are going to be using the client's 'future' side of their timeline. Just for a moment, think about where your future timeline is. Where do you place future events and fantastic things to come? Most people have their future towards their right or maybe in front of them. For this part of the Move, we gesture showing the client our left palm, which is held upwards and to our left (their right) a little higher than eye level.

This is doing a number of things. Firstly we are moving the client toward their future, and we are also directionalizing them to access the 'visual-create' part of the mind using the NLP eye-accessing cues. The eyes are a direct link to the brain as they are attached to the visual cortex via the optic nerve. We all make pictures in our mind's eye, are able to hear audio inside our mind, to feel different emotions and recall tactile experiences, and we often talk to ourselves. These aspects: visual, auditory, kinesthetic (emotions and tactile touch), and self-talk can also be related to where our eyes go to in order to 'search' for the correct experience.

This is not an exact science and there are a number of variations, however, we mostly search slightly upwards when trying to access images or pictures, laterally when accessing auditorily, down to our own right when accessing emotions or tactile experiences, and to our own left when talking to ourselves. For the visual level and the auditory senses, left generally indicates a memory is being accessed and right means imagination. So if someone is looking up and to their left, we say that they are recalling or remembering a picture, and if up to their right, that they are creating a picture. If their eyes move laterally to their left, they are recalling a sound, and if they glance laterally to their right, they are creating a sound. Again, these are generalizations.

When using this in the Coaching Pattern, we only need concern ourselves with guiding our client's eyes towards their 'visual create' space. This is likely to be up and to their right. This means that we, as the change worker, gesture with our left hand upwards with our palm facing towards their face slightly higher than eye level, we are leading them to raise their eyes to their 'visual create' space and at the same time we are asking them, "How do you want to be different?" We are in fact asking them

120

to create a picture, to make an image of exactly how they want to be when this problem is not an issue for them any more. And we are doing it totally on the unconscious level for them.

We are aware that our body language is 55% of our communication, so the gestures we make with our hands and arms can be large, over the top, superbly clear, and your client will easily follow your lead. You can also tilt your head and body to the right and then the left, utilizing everything you have to speak to you client on the unconscious level.

At this time, your tone of voice and energy level has to shift too. Using a faster tempo of speech, a more upbeat energy and a shift in tone also indicates a change to the unconscious mind. Remember mirror neurons? These are the neurons that light up in a similar way when we see someone else act in a particular fashion or move in a certain way. If I, as coach, ask this question: "How do you want to be different?" in a very low-key, somewhat bored manner, I am likely to get a very different answer than if I ask it in a much more up-tempo way. Obviously, you need to adjust your level of energy so that it is appropriate to the desired outcome. For example, if you know that the client wants to be calmer, then we may shift on our chair, take a nice breath, and ask in a calm manner how they would like to be different. Having the flexibility to adjust our own state is key and will lead the client to be able to access their state more readily.

So let's review the second step of dissociating from the Problem State, or in the Coaching Pattern: the Move.

Ask, "That's how you've been.... How do you want to be different?" At the same time sweep your right hand away to your right (the client's left) and then raise your left hand, palm facing the client, up slightly higher than their eye level, on their right. As we ask about how they want to be different, we shift our energy, voice tone and breathing, to help lead them into accessing that state.

Now we have dissociated them from the problem and started to help them access the desired Resource State. The next step is to associate them fully into the Resource State. As always, there are a number of factors to take into consideration here, particularly the level of association that the client is experiencing. It is vital to use your calibration skills in order to assess the level of association (or not) that your client is experiencing. You may find that simply by asking them how they want to be different immediately associates them into their desired state; in this case, congratulations: they have fast tracked into feeling that positive emotion and your job is much easier. On the other hand, they may have given you the word of the label that represents the emotion they desire, but it is clear that they have not yet fully associated into feeling or experiencing it. It is vitally important that the client associates fully and completely into the desired state, thereby lighting up the neurological areas associated with the positive feeling.

Let's say for example that your client has said that they would like to feel calm. You notice that when they first say that word "calm," they say it in a relaxed voice, while shifting in that chair to sink deeper into the comfort, and they take a nice deep breath and smile; you could begin to make the assumption that they are beginning to associate into calmness. If you see a shift such as this, a complete change in their physiology, voice tone, breathing and facial expression, then I would suggest that you move quickly to the next question and say, "And as you are feeling calm...think back to that old thing and notice how it is different now!"

So there you are as the coach; you have just stated, "That's how you've been..." while sweeping the client's problem to their left and into their past, followed by "...how do you want to be different?" and holding up your left palm toward them. You pause with a sense of expectation, and you raise your eyebrows inquiringly.

And they say, "I want to feel confident...", but this time they don't look confident. In fact, they don't even appear to be confident that they want to feel confident. Here's the next step of the Coaching Pattern: you take your left hand with its palm facing them, and you gently push it toward them, as if you are literally pushing confidence into them. As you do this, you ask, "And what's it like when you're feeling confident?"

Notice the hypnotic language in this simple statement; the embedded command, "You're feeling confident." And of course you are saying this in a confident tone of voice, so that their mirror neurons are beginning to fire off that sense of confidence.

And you see a shift, perhaps only a small shift, but nevertheless a shift. They look a little more confident. And you say to them, "Where do you feel that confidence in your body?"

This contains more hypnotic language; after all, you are presupposing that they are feeling confident in their body. By presupposing this, you invite them to go inside and look for it; when you look for a feeling, you will almost certainly find it, whether it was that before or not. The simple act of looking for a feeling creates it.

But they are still not sure. Perhaps they say something like, "Well, I guess I feel it in my chest...?" Now they have begun moving in the right direction, the snowball has started to roll downhill, and all you need to do is to give it another gentle push. You will say something like, "That's right, you DO feel it in your chest, and when you're feeling it in your chest, whereabouts in your chest are you feeling it now?"

So we are validating their feeling: "That's right, you DO..." We are affirming their experience and at the same time, giving an embedded command, "...you're feeling it in your chest...", and finally you are sending them on another search: "...whereabouts in your chest are you feeling it now?"

And we can continue in this way. You will take anything and everything that they give to you that suggests confidence, and you will amplify it and feed it back to them. The more you do this, the more confident they will feel, and the more confident they feel, the more signs of confidence they will provide to you, and the more signs of confidence they provide to you, the more you will have to feed back to them. And so on, a virtuous circle of confidence!

The final step, the Collapse, is the simplest of all. After all, you now have the context and trigger in which they experience the problem, and you have them fully associated into a powerful Resource State. Now comes the final question triggering the collapse of the resource and the problem:

"And as you're feeling that confidence now, take a look at that old issue and notice how it's different..."

If you have a more specific trigger – perhaps they experience the problem whenever they see their boss frown – you can direct the resource more specifically: "As you feel a sense of confidence now, see your boss's frown and notice how it's different..."

So this is the outline of the conversational Meta Pattern, otherwise known as the Coaching Pattern. We can loop through this pattern any number of times, so although each loop may only make a small change in the problem, the cumulative effect can be enormous.

Chapter Eleven:

The Hypnotic Meta Pattern

In this chapter we will discuss how the Meta Pattern can be used in all hypnosis sessions. Of course, hypnosis sessions often use NLP patterns and techniques, and as such the previous chapter describing how NLP patterns follow the Meta Pattern are applicable.

We hold the belief that the NLP patterns are hypnotic; after all, if your client is seeing a circle on the floor (Circle of Excellence), experiencing catalepsy (the Visual Squash) or seeing images on a movie screen (the V-K Dissociation), then they have accessed their unconscious mind and are exhibiting classic hypnotic phenomena!

What happens if you are doing more of a classical hypnosis session when you are inducing a deep trance and giving direct suggestions? How does the Meta Pattern apply then?

The answer is quite simple. When doing any sort of change work, even direct suggestions while in trance, it is important that you are specific as to the context of change work. The context of the change work is the place or circumstance that leads the clients to experience the problem, which is to say, it is the place where you will find the precise trigger for the problem. In order to make any long lasting changes with your client, it is essential to find this trigger moment: the specific thing that your client is seeing/hearing/touching that sets off the negative pattern of behavior. This is just as important when doing classical hypnosis as it is when doing any NLP patterns.

The more accurate you can be in finding the trigger moment, then the more precisely you can attach the direct suggestions to the trigger later in the process. This is what leads to effective change work.

Therefore, before you lead your client into trance, you should always explore the context in which they want to change. This may be a particular place, a particular time, when they are with particular people, or when they are doing particular activities. And within that context, what are the specific triggers that cause them to lose control over their feelings or behaviors? By doing this, you are utilizing the first step of the Meta Pattern: associating them into the context of the problem, calibrating to the unconscious body language, observing their state, finding the precise trigger (or triggers), and lighting up the neurological network that is associated with their problem.

The second step of the Meta Pattern is to dissociate from the Problem State. This is very easily done in classical hypnosis via the induction. Whether you are using a progressive relaxation, the Elman Induction, a confusion induction or any of the wide variety of inductions out there, when you lead your client into trance, the induction is likely to take them out of their Problem State and into a different state, for example, a state relaxation!

There are of course additional ways to dissociate your client from the Problem State that are often used in conjunction with an induction. In my practice I will usually sit with my client in one area of the office while talking about the problem (and beginning the process of change by getting them into step one of the Meta Pattern). Once we are ready to begin some formal trance work, I will ask the client to "come and sit in the change chair." Here I am utilizing one of the fastest ways to change someone's state…movement! By asking the client to stand up and walk to a different area of the office and to sit in the "relaxation" or "change" chair, I have intentionally got them to change their physiognomy and therefore their state. We can then begin the formal hypnosis with any induction, thus adding to the dissociation. Deepeners such as imagining walking down a beautiful staircase or classic deepening suggestions like "every breath you take takes you deeper" add to the dissociation, as do convincers such as heavy legs or eye lock.

You are now ready to move into Step Three: associate into the Resource State. This is the point in the hypnotic trance where you may be doing a guided visualization with embedded suggestions, a classic such as "the Inner Control Room," or work with symbols and metaphors. Whichever you are using, it is important to remember that you are allowing the unconscious mind to gather resources and are intentionally enhancing and building this state within your client's neurology.

If you are using direct suggestion, you can begin to associate the client into the Resource State using suggestions such as "You are feeling confident," or whatever the suggestions are. It's important to realize that because your client is in trance, they are highly suggestible, but this suggestibility lies mainly in the unconscious mind. The unconscious mind is less concerned with the words that it hears, and more concerned with the tonality of those words. So if you are giving a command such as, "You are feeling confident!" you need to say it in a very confident way to give their unconscious mind direction.

Finally, you do step four, the Collapse, by linking the resource to the original trigger for the problem. This is such a key step to making effective change.

It is fairly easy for us to help our client get into an amazing state by building up a resource and helping them to feel good. However, if we allow them to come out of trance and to leave our office having only done this, then the work is, in effect, incomplete. The truth of the matter is that your client will go back to their real world experience; they will go back into the exact same contexts and will experience the exact same triggers. They will go back to work and see their boss's face, or will be waiting for their turn to present at the Monday meeting, or will think about taking a flight. If we haven't attached a new resource to the precise trigger, then their old and familiar pattern with simply fire off again. We are in the business of helping the client to rewire their brain, to link together the new resource and the old trigger so the client has a new way to behave, a new pathway that fires off just as readily as their old one did, but his time taking them to a resourceful outcome.

Of course, just running through this pattern once only begins the process, and to make this new connection strong and robust, to make the new pathway the preferred one, to make this the superhighway to feeling good or confident, we need to cycle through this part of the pattern a number of times to ensure that these two neurological networks are really linked together.

This is a perfect place for using direct suggestions. As hypnotists, we know that we can repeat suggestions many times and the client's unconscious mind enjoys the repetition. Now we just need to repeat the suggestion and link it each time with the trigger: "You are feeling confident as you see your boss's face." "You are feeling relaxed as you think about taking a calm flight," etc.

If you are using a more indirect method of hypnosis, then the Meta Pattern still applies. One of our favorite techniques is "the Dreaming Arm." For this example, we will assume that we have already associated the client into the Problem State, found

128

the trigger(s) and then asked the client to "come and sit in the change chair."

From here we are likely to do an induction that involves asking which hand feels "something different." I am intentionally hoping to evoke some arm levitation here. Once the hand is beginning to move, I will give the unconscious mind an instruction such as "Now just allow your unconscious mind to go through all your memories, your experiences, and find all the times when you are feeling really confident, and each time your unconscious finds an example where you are feeling really confident, your hand will begin to move upwards…allow yourself to fully and completely feel just how good it feels to feel confident as your hand begins its uplifting journey towards feeling confident now." This is step three of the Meta Pattern, associating into the Resource State. We are trusting that the unconscious mind is very quickly accessing and building a big associated Resource State for the client. From here, when the hand has reached its destination or stops moving, we suggest that a "dream" or "symbol" will appear for the client. Here, we are layering up the Resource State.

The Collapse comes when we suggest that: "As your hand begins its journey back down, your unconscious mind is placing all these wonderful resources in exactly the right place in order to make this change for you now." If you have gone through all the steps of the Meta Pattern, including finding the trigger, then you, as the hypnotist, can also continue to suggest the precise contexts and triggers where the resources are being linked.

Having the Meta Pattern clearly in mind to guide the hypnotic process gives us the road map necessary for change on a deep unconscious level.

Chapter Twelve:

The Self-Coaching Pattern

As always in our NLP Mastery Series, we show you how to use the pattern for self coaching; after all, what's the point in having to run off to find your coach each time you find yourself feeling something you don't want to feel, doing something you don't want to do, or indeed not doing something that you want to do.

Dealing with Negative Feelings

We all have times in our lives when we have to deal with negative feelings. Perhaps you feel nervous when you have to speak to somebody you don't know. Perhaps you feel afraid when you have to give a speech in public; after all, it is widely reported as the biggest fear most people face. Perhaps there are people or events that make you feel angry. Maybe you even get down or depressed sometimes.

First of all, we need to make a distinction between emotions that are useful and those that are not. All our emotions are given to us for a reason; when you feel anger, your body is telling you it is ready to protect you by fighting, and when you feel fear, your body is telling you it is ready to run! Sometimes these feelings are appropriate; perhaps you need that kind feeling to give you the strength to defend yourself from physical or emotional attack. This is a useful fear, one that helps us to get out of a situation that is potentially dangerous.

But sometimes those emotions do not serve a useful purpose. Perhaps you get angry because a child accidentally broke a plate, or you get so afraid before your sales presentation that you can barely speak. Neither of these emotions is serving you well, and you're likely better off without them.

The first step to changing is recognizing when you are feeling these emotions, and there are a number of ways you can do this. For example, you may think about those times and places when you feel less than your best; where are you when these take place? Who were you with? What was happening? By noticing common threads, you will begin to identify the triggers that make you feel this way. Perhaps it's a certain place, perhaps it's a certain person, or perhaps it's a certain event.

Associating into the problem or Present State: When you have identified these triggers, imagine you are back there in that place, with that person, or in an event. See what you see, and hear what you hear, and you should begin to feel a little of that same feeling.

Dissociating from the Present State: the simplest way of dissociating from the state is to consider how you will be as a person when this is no longer an issue for you. How will you be different knowing that you can change in this way, knowing that you can choose to be more resourceful? Consider what is really important to you about being in that place, with that person, or at that event. For example, if you get overly nervous giving a sales presentation, ask yourself what is important to you about giving the presentation: succeeding at work obviously. And what's important to you about that? Getting that promotion, getting paid more? And what is important to you about that? Providing for your family? And when you're providing for your family, who are you then as a person, a provider?

If you find it difficult to think of this new you, think instead of somebody, real or fictional, who would handle this situation better. Either way, begin to build up a picture of this new you, or this other person. See them in your mind's eye as if they were standing in front of you.

Associating to the Resource State: When you have that picture very clearly in front of you, that new you or ideal self, imagine stepping or floating into that and feeling how good that feels.

Because you can do this exercise before you ever get into the real situation, you can practice it a number of times. Imagine seeing that image again in front of you, floating into it and allowing those good feelings to double. Imagine seeing that image again in front of you, floating into it and allowing those good feelings to double again. Really build this positive state so it feels strong and powerful and real to you.

The Collapse: Now, in order to do the Collapse, we have to attach the positive state to the trigger or context. Once more, step or float into that positive state, and as you feel it building up in your body, imagine you are back in the context where you previously experienced the problem. Notice how it's different.

Repeat this step a number of times to condition your new response to the trigger or context.

This pattern also works with unwanted behaviors, because at the end of the day those behaviors are driven by inappropriate states. Therefore, all you have to do is to identify the contexts and triggers (places, people or events) where you behave the way you don't want to behave. Associate back into those contexts by seeing what you see and hearing what you hear when you are there. You should begin to feel the urge to do that unwanted behavior again! (Associate into the Problem State)

Now think about how you would like to be instead. What would you be doing? How would your behavior be different? What kind of person will you be when you are able to do this instead? (Dissociate from the Problem State)

How will you be feeling when you are that person? Notice what it's like when you're feeling that in your body. (Associate into the Resource State)

As you begin to feel that feeling, vividly imagine that you are back in the context: seeing what you're seeing, and hearing what you're hearing. Notice how it's different. (The Collapse) Again, repeat this step as many times as needed until the new behavior begins to condition and feel natural.

Installing New Behaviors

Sometimes the issue is not how we feel, or what we do, but rather what we don't do. This type of problem manifests itself in such things as the motivation of procrastination.

The easiest way to run the Meta Pattern on this type of issue is using the resource of "How you will feel when you have done the task?" For example, how will you feel when you have filed your taxes? How will you feel when you have written the next chapter of your book, or if that doesn't do it for you, who will you be when you have finished your book?

So here's the pattern again:

Associate into the problem or Present State: Think about the context or situation (places, people or events) where you feel unmotivated, or where you procrastinate. Imagine you are in this situation, seeing what you see and hearing what you hear.

You should begin to notice that lethargic non-motivation or procrastination creeping upon you!

Dissociate from the Problem State: Begin to consider how you will be as a person when that task is done: your taxes are filed; your book is written; the lawn is mowed; the washing up is done.

Associate into the Resource State: Whatever the task might be, begin to strongly imagine you've finished that task and notice how good that feels. Allow that good feeling to build up in your body.

The Collapse: As that good feeling builds in your body, imagine the context or situation where you need that motivation, and notice how it's different.

Using the Meta Pattern 'In the Moment'

Sometimes you don't get the opportunity to plan in advance. A situation leaps upon you and you find yourself reacting, perhaps feeling bad or behaving inappropriately. This is a great technique based upon John Overdurf's self-coaching pattern that is also a demonstration of the Meta Pattern.

Associate into the Problem State: This is the easiest step, as you already there!

Dissociate from the Problem State: This often seems like the most difficult step. Once you begin feeling bad, it often seems difficult to get out of the cycle of negative thoughts and negative feelings. In fact, it's quite an easy step because of a new logical rule called the 90-second rule.

The 90-second rule essentially says that most emotions we feel last no more than 90 seconds unless we keep them going by thinking about the problem. I'm sure you've had this experience when somebody has said something or done something that upsets you. You feel angry about it, and you start to tell yourself, "I can't believe they did that, it was just plain nasty, they obviously don't like me, what's wrong with them, maybe it's something wrong with me…" and so on, round and round and round. Each of these thoughts makes you feel a little worse, and each time those negative feelings increase, you think more negative thoughts. It's a vicious circle that seems to last forever.

The easiest way to step out of this circle of negativity is to stop thinking the thoughts. Once the thought stop, the feelings have another 90 seconds before they too dissipate and disappear. This begs the question: How do you stop thinking the thoughts? After all, they seem to come all by themselves. The answer is to dissociate from the feeling, because it's the feeling that drive thoughts. How do we dissociate from the feeling? It's actually simple: we turn it from an emotion ('anger') into a somatic feeling in the body ('a feeling in my chest'), and then we begin to abstract it so it becomes even less like an emotion ('like a black rock in my chest, the size of a baseball').

Once you have turned the emotion into a mere feeling, and the feeling into a descriptive metaphor, all you have to do is to wait for 90 seconds, noticing how it changes as time goes by: "It's beginning to get smaller. That's interesting: the colors are changing from black to gray… It's beginning to fade… Wow, it's gone."

When the feeling has gone, you are dissociated from the problem. Now it's time for you to find a good resource. Once again, let's go to the idea of values: What's everything else that's important to you about being in this place, at this time, that you haven't been considering up until now? And of all those things that are important, what comes to mind as the *most* important? Who will you be as a person when you have that as part of who you are?

Let's take the example of Dan, a salesman who is required to make cold calls. Dan usually feels fine hearing the frequent "no's," but occasionally, because he has struck out a number of times in a row, or perhaps just because it's been a long day, he starts to feel anxious about the next call, and this feeling of anxiousness inevitably leads to another failure, making him feel even more anxious, and he can end up with totally wasted day.

Associate into the Problem State: Dan begins to pay attention to the feeling of anxiety and is able to identify it as soon as it starts and before it snowballs into something larger.

Dissociate from the Problem State: As soon as he feels it, he locates it in his body (usually in his chest and throat). He notices the size, shape, color, movement and temperature of the feeling, and begins to notice how those change over time: how the feeling moves around in his body, grows or shrinks, changes shape or color and so on. In 90 seconds or less, it is gone.

Associate into the Resource State: Dan now asks himself what is everything that is really important about him making these calls. He realizes he believes in his product and believes that it will make a positive difference in the lives of his customers. He remembers his wife and young baby at home that he is providing for. As he thinks about these values, a warm glow begins to move through him.

The Collapse: As he feels this new resourceful state, he picks up the phone and dials his next prospect.

Using the Meta Pattern for self-coaching presents a number of challenges. The first of these is becoming familiar with our own emotional states. How many times do you actually go inside and check how you're feeling? In order to achieve self-mastery, it is first necessary to achieve self-knowledge. Go inside now and check how you're feeling. Are you energized or tired? Do things appear clear to you, or are you confused? How are you feeling? Get used to checking on yourself on a regular basis.

The second challenge to using the Meta Pattern for self-coaching is being able to dissociate from the state. Remember, states and emotions are all provided to you to give you the best chance of surviving: you get angry when you have to fight, scared when you have to run, and you fall in love when you meet your soulmate! But sometimes these feelings come at the wrong time and you want to choose another way of feeling. All you have to do is wait for 90 seconds without throwing logs on the fire by thinking negative thoughts. Just allow your mind to rest on the feeling as a sensation in your body and notice how it changes as the seconds tick by. By the time a minute and a half have gone, so has the feeling.

The next challenge is recognizing that you can actually choose to feel the way you want to feel. You can choose to feel confident. You can choose to feel happy. You can choose to feel calm. Just see a picture of yourself, life-sized in front of you, feeling that way. Then step into the picture and begin to pay attention to the good feelings inside. The more you pay attention to these feelings, the stronger they become. And the more you practice this, the more natural it becomes.

Once you have mastered the skill of letting go of unwanted emotions and choosing the emotions that you want to feel instead, the rest is easy. Just feel great, positive emotions as you step into the next adventure in your life!

Chapter Thirteen:

The Meta Pattern in Daily Life

The Meta Pattern is not relegated to only the coaching space. It is at the heart of all successful influence. It appears continuously in our day-to-day lives. This is the familiar structure that underlies all powerful communication that brings about emotional states.

The Meta Pattern in TV Commercials

The Meta Pattern is such a part of the fabric of our lives that we are often unaware of it on a conscious level. However, once we become aware of this cycle of change, we are able to identify examples of it throughout our daily lives. In fact, it can become so glaringly obvious that you may find that you begin to recognize it almost everywhere you look! It is a universal pattern that we can see in various forms from advertising to fairy tales, political speeches, movies and books.

Let's take advertising as a great example of the Meta Pattern, and in particular, commercials on the television.

You may have seen a classic advert for pain medication that follows this kind of scenario:

Lady holding her head, complaining of headache. There are loud noises around her, perhaps pneumatic drills in the street.

Scene changes to a man in a white coat in a laboratory.

Scene changes again: the lady is holding the bottle of pills and swallowing one.

In the final scene the lady is playing with her noisy, excited children in the yard.

The commercial runs perhaps a minute, allowing us to fully experience the entire cycle, and we can very clearly see how it follows the structure of the Meta Pattern:

Lady holding head, complaining of headache, with loud jarring noises around her. Our mirror neurons begin to fire off, we literally feel her pain (Step 1 – Associate into the Problem State).

Man in white coat in the lab (Step 2 – Dissociate from the Problem State).

Lady holds the bottle of pills and swallows one (Step 3 – Associate into the Resource State, in this case taking the medication).

Lady seen playing with her children (Step 4 – the collapse – we are taking the resource back to the initial Problem State and transforming it, by taking the tablet and getting rid of the headache).

Let's take a look at another ad, in this case a State Farm Insurance Commercial:

Accident Happens (Step 1 – Associate into the Problem)

Lady sings the "State Farm Song" (Step 2 – Dissociate from the Problem)

Money Arrives (Step 3 – Associate into the Resource)

Car gets fixed (Step 4 – the Collapse)

As you can see, these commercials are following the Meta Pattern very closely. Due to reaching out to a vast audience, the ads are unable to associate into events that are specific to each viewer, and instead rely on universal experiences: common experiences, thoughts or feelings that most people can associate to. In the above examples they rely on the fact that most of us will have experienced a headache, or a fender-bender.

The Meta Pattern in Stories

If we look at the structure of a simple fairy tale such as "Cinderella," we find that it follows the Meta Pattern. The story demonstrates how we often cycle through a few iterations of the pattern. Here is the basic outline:

Poor Cinderella is found scrubbing the floor at the behest of her ugly sisters and not allowed to go to the ball (Step 1 – associate into the Problem State).

Fairy Godmother arrives (Step 2 – dissociate from the problem).

Cinderella receives a gown, glass slippers, attends the ball and dances with the prince (Step 3 – associate into the Resource State).

As the clock strikes midnight, Cinderella leaves the ball and loses a glass slipper. She returns home, taking her experiences (resource) back with her to the place and context where she started (Step 4 – there is a small "collapse" as she is certainly different now than before).

...And the story continues through another cycle

The Prince brings the glass slipper to the house, but Cinderella is not allowed to try it, being banished to the kitchen (associate into the Problem State).

The Prince asks if there is anyone else in the house (dissociate from the problem).

Cinderella tries the slipper and it fits! (Associate into the Resource State).

They marry and live happily ever after (the Collapse).

It is a very very familiar cycle isn't it? In story and film we see the pattern occurring again:

The Wizard of Oz: The tornado takes Dorothy away – She travels the Yellow Brick Road where meets the Scarecrow, the Tin Man and the Cowardly Lion – after overcoming many trials she realizes that her power and strength come from within – she returns to Kansas renewed.

Casablanca: Rick is an unhappy expat in Casablanca – his ex-love Ilsa re-enters his life, and their love is rekindled, even though Ilsa is married and Rick gets to observe the nobility of Ilsa's husband, who is working against the Nazis – Rick regains his own nobility and releases Ilsa from her promise to him – Ilsa leaves and Rick realizes that it is better to have loved and lost than never to have loved at all.

The Matrix: Thomas Anderson (Neo) lives a normal life until Agent Smith arrives and starts to hunt him down – Morpheus helps Neo to escape and shows him 'the Matrix' – Neo becomes 'the One' and defeats Agent Smith – Neo returns to the Matrix to complete the battle.

Jane Eyre (Charlotte Bronte): Orphan Jane is sent to a school where she is mistreated – She becomes a governess – she falls in love with Mr. Rochester (loses him and finds him again) and discovers her personal power – she marries Mr. Rochester and finds happiness.

The Hobbit (J.R.R. Tolkein): Gandalf tells Bilbo that Middle Earth is in trouble and he has been chosen to help save it, they travel into the wilds with the dwarves who consider Bilbo to be more or less useless – Bilbo finds the ring – using the power of the ring, Bilbo helps the dwarves battle goblins and giant spiders, finally defeating the Dragon – Bilbo returns to the Shire with his newfound and hard-won experiences.

The Meta Pattern in Politics

Lets look at how the same pattern (associate into the Problem State, dissociate from the Problem State, associate into the Resource State and bring the resource back to the problem) is used in political speeches. If you choose to write a political speech, it is probably going to sound something like this:

"A vote for my opponent is a vote for somebody who intends to take us back into the dark ages by... [list all the problematic things your opponent intends to do, or has already done]...

But there's a better way...

Vote for me and I will leaders into a bright new future by... [list all the wonderful things that you intend to do, or have already done]...

The polls open soon, so go out and vote for progress..."

It's the same old story: associate into the problem, dissociate, associate to the resource, collapse by asking for their vote.

Putting aside any political ideology or rhetoric, any affiliation or political preference, let's just look at the structure of the speech, the states through which the politician is leading (or intending to lead) the listener. Here is an extract from President Obama's acceptance speech given in Chicago, Illinois in 2008:

I was never the likeliest candidate for this office. We didn't start with much money or many endorsements. (Associate into the Problem State)

Our campaign was not hatched in the halls of Washington. It began in the backyards of Des Moines and the living rooms of Concord and the front porches of Charleston. (Dissociate from the Problem State)

It was built by working men and women who dug into what little savings they had to give $5 and $10 and $20 to the cause. It grew strength from the young people who rejected the myth of their generation's apathy, who left their homes and their families for jobs that offered little pay and less sleep. It drew strength from the not-so-young people who braved the bitter cold and scorching heat to knock on doors of perfect strangers, and from the millions of Americans who volunteered and organized and proved (Associate into the Resource State)

...that more than two centuries later a government of the people, by the people, and for the people has not perished from the Earth. This is your victory. (The Collapse)

Here is an extract from one of Winston Churchill's most famous speeches, delivered to the House of Commons and the British People on June 4th, 1940. It clearly adheres to the structure of the Meta Pattern!

"Even thought large tracts of Europe and many old famous States have fallen or may fall into the grip of the Gestapo and all the odious apparatus of Nazi rule, (associate into the Problem State)

we shall not flag or fail. We shall go on to the end. (Dissociate from the Problem State)

We shall fight in France, we shall fight on the seas and the oceans, we shall fight with growing strength in the air, we shall defend our Island, whatever the cost may be. We shall fight on the beaches, we shall fight on the landing grounds, we shall fight in the fields and in the streets, we shall fight in the hills; (Associate into the Resource State)

We shall never surrender, (The Collapse)

and if, which I do not for a moment believe, this Island or a large part of it were subjugated and starving, (associate into the Problem State)

then our Empire beyond the seas, (dissociate from the Problem State)

armed and guarded by the British Fleet, would carry on the struggle, (associate into the Resource State)

until, in God's good time the New World, with all its power and might, steps forth to the rescue and the liberation of the old." (The Collapse)

Or how about the famous Gettysburg Address, given by Abraham Lincoln on November 18th, 1863.

"Four score and seven years ago our fathers brought forth on this continent a new nation, conceived in liberty and dedicated to the proposition that all men are created equal. Now we are engaged in a great civil war, testing whether that nation or any nation so conceived and so dedicated can long endure. (Associate into the Problem)

We are met on a great battlefield of that war. We have come to dedicate a portion of that field as final resting place for those who here gave their lives that nation might live. It is altogether fitting and proper that we should do this. (Dissociate from the Problem)

144

But, in a larger sense, we cannot dedicate, we cannot consecrate, we cannot hallow this ground. The brave men, living and dead who struggled here have consecrated it far above our poor power to add or detract. The world will little note nor long remember what we say here, bit it can never forget what they did here. It is for us the living rather to be dedicated here to the unfinished work, which they who fought here have thus far nobly advanced. It is rather for us to be here dedicated to the great task remaining before us – that from these honored dead we take increased devotion to that cause for which that gave the last full measure of devotion – (Associate into the Resource)

that we here highly resolve that these dead shall not have died in vain, that this nation under God shall have a new birth of freedom, and that government of the people, by the people and for the people shall not perish from the earth." (The Collapse)

We can see the same pattern being used over and over. Now, of course these are just extracts from these famous speeches. It is a great exercise to take a full transcript of the speech go through the entire document and see just how many times this speaker cycles through the four steps of the Meta Pattern.

Chapter Fourteen:

The Meta Pattern and Business

In the following chapters we will focus our attention on using the Meta Pattern within a business context. Because this book is primarily about the use of the Meta Pattern in coaching and change work, we will simply give an overview of how the framework provided by the Meta Pattern can be used in five different business contexts:

A negotiation
A sales pitch
A formal presentation
Sales copy writing
Goal-setting
Giving performance feedback

As context we will go through the four steps of the Meta Pattern, explaining how each relates to the specific business process. We will also give a brief real-world example (details have been changed for confidentiality reasons).

In each case we will follow the same basic pattern:

Associate into the Present State or Problem State: we will seek to discover what the specific audience needs and wants.

What problems are they having which they need to solve, or what do they want that they don't yet have? If we're speaking to one person, it should be relatively easy to discover this. If we are speaking to a group of people, it may be more difficult to gather all their wants and needs, and we may have to make some assumptions based upon what we know about them. Repeat these wants and needs back to them and obtain their agreement that these are indeed their issues.

Dissociate from the Present State or Problem State: the easiest way to do this is to present some information or data that is not specific to their particular problem, but has a bearing on it.

Associate into the Resource State or solution: this can often be achieved by talking about someone who has similar wants and needs, and who was able to resolve those using the solution you are just about to propose! Calibrate for their unconscious agreement.

Collapse: propose your solution. The benefits you will stress are the resolution of their problems, and will provide for their wants and needs. If you have obtained their agreement to steps one and three, there should be few objections at this step four. Close the deal.

Chapter Fifteen:

Negotiation or B2C Sales Pitch

There are two ways to think about a negotiation; it can be considered a zero-sum game in which there is a winner and a loser. Within this model my aim is to outmaneuver you by getting you to concede the greatest amount of territory, whilst conceding the least amount of territory myself. This is called a win-lose negotiation.

The second way to think about a negotiation is within a win-win framework. In this framework I seek to provide you with the greatest amount of value, at the least amount of cost to you. Of course, I will also be seeking to minimize my own costs. This may sound counter-intuitive, but it really isn't. In fact, it greatly simplifies the negotiation process.

Let's look at a simple example in the context of a Business to Consumer (B2C) sale for a high cost item, for example a car. This is often thought of as primarily a price negotiation.

Supposing I'm a used car salesman and you are a potential customer, who is interested in the blue Honda Civic that is sitting in my lot. In a win-lose negotiation, my aims as the salesman might include getting you to pay the maximum price for the vehicle and persuading you to pay for various extras such as an extended warranty, while providing you only the car and incurring as few additional costs as possible. Your aim as the customer is to pay as little as possible for the vehicle, to avoid being persuaded to pay for extras you don't really want or need, and getting the extras you do want thrown in for nothing, or at a nominal price. Within this frame the only way that I can win as salesman is by making you lose as customer.

Let's consider this within the light of the Meta Pattern. In the same way that we use the Meta Pattern in a coaching context, I will cycle through the steps several times during the sales process. The first step is to associate you into your Problem State, perhaps the fact that you don't own a car and catching public transportation is such a drag, or that the car you own is a bucket of rust that is just about to fall apart and cost you several thousand dollars in mechanic's fees.

Now I'm going to dissociate you from your problem of not owning a car by walking you around my lot, so you can look at the cars I have. At some point I noticed your eyes fixed on the beautiful blue Honda Civic.

Now I'm going to associate you into the Resource State. Here, the Resource State is how your life will be when you are the proud owner of this used blue Honda Civic. I'll show you the blue Honda Civic using all your representational systems of sight, hearing, feeling and of course smell; I'll let you look at it, sit in it, listen to the engine and the radio, smell the recently cleaned leather upholstery, and finally perhaps take you for a test drive. At the same time, I'll get you to imagine how awesome your life will be when you own it. When I see you have fallen in love with the car, I'm ready to move onto step four, the Collapse; I take you into the office to 'discuss terms.'

So now we have a problem (you don't have a car) and the resource or solution (you could be the proud owner of this used blue Honda Civic). The only thing required to match solution with problem is to overcome any pesky objections.

Each objection can itself be overcome by applying the Meta Pattern; the objection indicates the customer's Present State or Problem State. For example: "It seems very expensive..." might mean "I think I can get a better deal somewhere else," or "I'm not sure I have the budget for this." My next step as salesman will be to dissociate you from the problem, perhaps by showing you some objective information, and then associating you into a more positive Resource State: "Let me show you the Blue Book price for this baby... You will not find a better price anywhere else. You'll be really happy you bought this!" or "Let's talk about financing; take a look at these payment terms... This is actually going to reduce your monthly travel expenses... What are you going to do with all that extra money?"

Now you may think you're done. You've agreed to sign over your firstborn child to the finance company, but at least you have a car. But you're not so lucky; I'm ready to move into selling cycle two. The first part is to associate you into the problem: "Congratulations! Of course you'll be wanting the extended warranty... The problem with used cars is they don't come with a manufacturer's warranty..." And now into step two, dissociating from the problem: "Let me show you this extended warranty; it covers parts and labor for two years..." and rapidly moving into step three, associating into the resource or solution: "It provides complete peace of mind, knowing that you'll have trouble-free driving for a complete two years..." Finally, we move into step four, the Collapse; all we have to do is to overcome those pesky objections: "This week we have a special finance offer where you can roll the cost of the warranty into your car loan..."

And of course you'll want rust protection...

Contrast this with a win-win negotiation. My aim as a salesman is to add as much value as possible to your buying experience with as little cost to you as possible. Let's consider this within the context of the Meta Pattern. My first step is to associate you into the Problem State. However, within the win-win frame, the Present State or Problem State is not that you don't have a car, and it's not that I haven't yet made a sale, it's that we (you and I) have not yet come to a mutually agreeable arrangement. Therefore, my opening remarks are not going to be about the pain of using public transportation, or the fact that your gearbox is just about to drop out of your old clunker. They're going to be about how I intend to make it easy for us to agree on a deal by satisfying all your needs in a way that's fair for me.

Now onto step two of the Meta Pattern; dissociating you and me both, us, from our lack of a deal. In order to do, so I'm going to lay out the pieces of value that I believe will be important to you, and the pieces of value that are important to me, and then seek to reconcile them. Your pieces of value might include: getting a fair price, getting other value-added services that you perceive as being important, being delighted with your purchase, and finally finding an honest used-car salesman who you can come back to in the future. My pieces of value might include: getting a fair price for my vehicle, providing any other value-added services that are important to you as the customer, having you as a delighted customer send me referral business, and having you return to me as a future customer when you're looking for your next car. When considered in this way, the interests of salesmen and customer are closely aligned; by agreeing a fair price, we both win; by providing you with the value-added services that you want, we both win; by creating enough value for you that you are delighted with your purchase, we both win; and by your wanting to come back the next time you need a car because you are so delighted with your experience, we both win.

Now onto step three: I have to associate you into the Resource State. So I tell you about our price guarantee, that we regularly survey the prices being charged by other dealerships to make sure we are at least as competitive. In fact, we find we can beat other dealerships' prices because we focus on service and have the highest rate of return business in the industry. We can therefore offer a price guarantee that if you can find a comparable vehicle at a cheaper price anywhere else we will match that price and give you a check for $200. Hopefully you now believe you're getting a fair price, and in any case you know you will not regret the purchase because you can come back and claim your discount and a $200 check if necessary. I'm not going to go through all of the value-added services, extended warranty, rust protection and so on, I'm going to lay out the advantages and cost of each, and because you are now beginning to trust me I am going to make a recommendation on each of them; and each time I tell you you don't need one of them, my credibility increases. And now I am going to ask you for something in return: I'm going to tell you that the blue Honda Civic you are buying is such a great car I want the opportunity to take it as a trade-in when you're buying your next car. And I also want you to recommend me to your friends, which means that I want you to be absolutely delighted as a customer. I write my cell phone number on the back of my business card and if there is anything, and I mean anything, that you need or that you're unhappy with, please call me. And a week from now, and a month from now, I'm going to call you and make sure that you are delighted with the car.

By doing this I have associated you into a bright future where you are delighted with the car, totally comfortable with the price, and have all the value-added features you actually want.

Now on to step four of the Meta Pattern, the Collapse. If I've done my job correctly up until now, the Collapse is easy; everything is agreed and we sign the paperwork. Now, of course I don't mean to imply that I wouldn't show you the car, or take you for a test drive, of course I would. But these now take a different function; I'm no longer seeking to make you fall in love with the car (although you may) so you will feel its loss if you don't buy it. Instead I am associating you into this comfortable future where you own the car you want, at the price you want, with the extras you want, and with the support you want.

At first sight, each of these approaches may seem to be similar. After all, the salesman is discussing the same things: the car, the value-added extras including the warranty and the financing package, and so on. So what has really changed? Well, if you have ever worked in sales you'll know that the moment of truth, especially for less experienced salesmen, is the close or ask where you actually have to ask for the sale, or ask for money. This can feel uncomfortable for the salesman, which not only makes his job less pleasant than it might be, but is also communicated to the customer through the salesman's unconscious body language; at some level the customer realizes, "This guy is uncomfortable with this price, what's wrong with it?" There are two parts to this discomfort: the first is that the salesman views the negotiation as a win-lose and by asking for the sale the salesman is 'winning,' and thereby making the customer 'lose.' The second discomfort is that if the customer says "no," then the salesman loses. Either way somebody loses and the salesman's unconscious mind recognizes that, and is uncomfortable as a result.

In the win-win frame, there is no losing. I am seeking to add as much value as I possibly can to your experience. If something does not add value to your experience, I simply don't do it; for example, I don't try and sell you the warranty if that is not going to be valuable to you. If you don't want the warranty, and I don't try to persuade you to take the warranty, you win, but I win as well because you have a better experience and will send me more business in the longer term either by referring your friends, or by returning the next time you want a car. Even if we can't agree on a price that is fair to both of us for the blue Honda Civic, it's still a win-win because you've had a positive experience, and I have gained a potential referral source as a result. You may even return later on when you can't find a better price anywhere else.

Other Business Negotiations

Many years ago I was involved in a negotiation between a company and a labor union. Each side had their entrenched position and they had reached deadlock. The company was arguing for reduction-in-force and pay freezes for the remaining workers. The labor union was prepared to accept nothing more than a hiring freeze, and wanted a new contract including step pay rises in return.

The company's argument went as follows: the company had traditionally been profitable but now was facing financial difficulties (associate into the Problem State); here are the financial statements showing the company has to improve profitability and cash flow otherwise it will go out of business (dissociate from the Problem States by focusing on the numbers); making these reductions-in-force and temporary pay freezes will make the company viable once again, the remaining workers will keep their jobs (associate the Resource or Solution State); and in a few years when the company is out of the woods, pay raises will be reinstated (Collapse).

The labor union's argument went as follows: we the workers have foregone pay raises for the last two years (associate into the Problem State); we understand the company is facing financial difficulties, but these difficulties have been caused by bad management and it is not appropriate for the workers to bear all the consequences (dissociate from the problem by deflecting the blame); the management can find other ways of cost-cutting, for example, cutting management compensation and shareholder dividends (associate into the resource or

154

solution); once management has found alternative solutions, we can discuss a new contract (Collapse).

The reason management and the labor-union were deadlocked was because, while they were both using the Meta Pattern to seek a solution, they were each using a different version of the Meta Pattern. They did not agree on the nature of the problem (for management it was a financial problem while for the labor-union it was the lack of pay raises). They did not agree on the relevant information to be considered (for management it was the financial statements, for the labor-union it was the broader narrative of how the company came to be in the current position). They did not agree on the solution (for management it was reduction-in-force and further pay freezes, for the labor-union it was seeking other expense reductions and cash flow improvements). Because there was virtually no ground between the management and labor-union, no progress could be made.

To make a long story short, the solution came about by identifying a third meta pattern, which incorporated the concerns of management, shareholders, and workers as follows:

The problem: the company is currently generating both insufficient profit and insufficient cash flow to satisfy the needs of the various stake-holders: the shareholders, creditors, and employees, both management and white-collar as well as blue-collar workers.

Dissociate from the problem using relevant information and data: current financial data including balance sheets, profit and loss statements, and cash flow statements; pipeline and financial projections; banking and loan arrangements; shareholder cash flow needs.

Associate into the Resource State: all the stakeholders want a profitable and financially viable company to satisfy their needs; the shareholders wish to preserve their wealth, lenders and creditors wish to preserve security of their loans, management wish to preserve their management positions, employees wish to preserve their jobs and compensation and benefits. The solution was some way of achieving this Resource State in a balanced way.

What ended up happening was that the family shareholders decided to sell the company to management partly using venture-capital funds, and partly using an employee stock ownership plan (ESOP). They were happy because they converted their shares in a financially shaky company into cash, preserving their wealth.

The lenders and creditors were happy because they were paid off by the venture capital funds, guaranteeing the value of their loans by converting them back into cash.

Management was happy because they got to preserve their management roles, and now had upside potential because they owned part of the company. As a result, they reduced their own compensation, improving the company's cash flow position.

The workers were happy because they received a future ownership stake in the company through the ESOP. This gave them both a financial interest as well as a say in the running of the company. As a result, the labor-union agreed to some early retirements and signed a new contract with more flexible work terms.

The important thing to realize this is that it was the changing of the Meta Pattern to include the problems perceived by all sides, the information available to all sides, and the resources available to all sides that turned the negotiation from a confrontational win-lose to a cooperative win-win.

So, once more to summarize the Meta Pattern in negotiations using the win-win frame:

Associate into the Present State. The Present State is that we haven't yet reached an agreement favorable to both of us. We associate our negotiating partner into this state by saying something equivalent to, "I really want to do business with you, I want you to be absolutely delighted with the relationship."

Dissociate from the Present State. We do this by literally laying our cards on the table, so both sides can see what is important to the other. We do this by saying something equivalent to, "These are the things that are important to me in this agreement. Some of these things are not going to cost you anything. Some of them will cost you something and we need to agree a price that is fair to both of us. These are the things that I believe will be important to you. Some of them will cost me nothing and I will be delighted to provide them to you even if we don't reach agreement on the bigger picture. There may also be other things which are important to you, and I really want to understand what those might be, so I can meet your expectations."

Associate into the Resource State. We do this by future pacing our negotiating partner into the state they will feel when they actually have the things that are important to them. We do this by saying something equivalent to, "So I hear you say that timing is important on this project. If I provide a report to you on Wednesday morning, how will you feel about that?"

The Close. Within the win-win frame, the Collapse becomes extremely easy because most of the negotiating points have been dealt with in step three. In fact, we don't move on to the Collapse until we all feel sure that all points have been dealt with. If there is an objection when we move to the close then we have missed something in an earlier step and we need to go back.

Chapter Sixteen:

Using the Meta Pattern in a Sales Pitch

This chapter will consider how you can use the Meta Pattern when preparing a more formal sales presentation, or when meeting with a prospective client. In this case the Meta Pattern will follow the following outline:

The Present State or problem: this will be an identification of the prospect's needs and wants in relation to your product or service. Where are they now? What is not working for them? What do they want to change? What frustrations do they have? What keeps them awake at night?

Dissociating from the Problem State: presenting them with information on your company, service or product can do this. Who are you, and who is your company? What makes you special and distinguishes you from your competitors? Make sure that whatever attributes you list are things that they value! What industries and segments do you serve? Whatever industry or segment you talk about, make sure they are in it! What type of clients do you work with? Again, make sure they are this type of client!

Associating into the Resource State or solution: this essentially answers the question "How can you add value to their business?" The easiest way of doing that is to talk about how you help your existing clients; the problems you help them to resolve and the benefits they achieve as a result. Using the principles in this book, you can begin to associate them into how they, or their business, will be different when they engage with you to help them. For example, you can shift pronouns to use 'you,' and also shift into present tense languaging. Talking about the client you have helped in this way allows you to begin to calibrate whether or not they are 'buying-in' to your proposal. The simplest way to do this is to subtly nod your head when you're talking about the benefits your product or service provides to the clients, and see if they nod back. If they do, then they are unconsciously agreeing with what you're saying. Make sure you do this in a subtle way! You cannot move on to the final step in the Meta Pattern until you see them beginning to agree on an unconscious level.

The Collapse: this is when you begin to apply the service to their specific needs, when you present your formal or informal proposal to them. Because you have obtained unconscious agreement during the previous step, there should be few objections left to overcome at this final stage other than perhaps pricing. A simple yet effective way of dealing with the pricing issue is to offer them different service options or payment terms with different pricing levels.

Example:

I have been asked to make a proposal to a company for consulting services relating to their corporate structure. I meet with Matt, the CFO, to discuss their needs. They are a privately owned pharmaceutical company and want to set up operations in Switzerland. As we discuss their needs, Matt impresses upon me that they want to operate in the simplest way possible because Matt wishes to avoid any complications in his operating structure. I outline the range of options they have, stressing the simplest one. I promise Matt I'll get him a formal proposal.

Next I receive a phone call from one of the principal owners of the company, Wesley, who asks me to summarize my conversation with Matt. As I go through the options I have described to Matt, Wesley begins to ask me detailed questions about the more complex (but financially more efficient) structure. I realize I now have a significant difference of opinion between different stakeholders in the company, which I need to address as part of the proposal.

My proposal is going to follow this outline:

Associate into the Problem State: as far as Matt is concerned, the major problem is the potential complexity of any structure, but as far as Wesley is concerned the major problem is financial inefficiency. Therefore, the Present State or 'problem' that I have to address is how to develop structure that is financially efficient, yet operationally simple.

Dissociate from the Problem State: to do this I'm going to talk about my capabilities and the capabilities of my organization. I am going to stress our expertise in structuring international operations, and our experience in dealing with privately owned companies within the pharmaceutical industry. I want to explain that what makes us different is our ability to develop structures that meet the varied needs of our clients, from operational simplicity through financial efficiency.

Associated to the Resource State: I am going to list some of our privately held clients in the pharmaceutical industry, and perhaps give brief case histories of how we help them to develop their international business structures, talking about operational simplicity and financial efficiency.

160

The proposal itself is going to outline my proposed structure, giving details on the cost savings that can be achieved, and also how we can provide 'turnkey' implementation of the structure, and modify the company's systems to allow easy operation of the structure.

Once I have prepared my proposal, I go to the company to present it in person. As I go through the proposal, I'm very mindful of the distinct interests of Matt and Wesley. James, the CEO, who I have not previously met, so I don't know his preferences, joins us at the meeting. As I go through the proposal, I talk about the importance of financial efficiency, making sure that Wesley is in agreement, and then about the importance of operational simplicity, making sure that Matt is in agreement. At the same time, I'm watching for James' reaction. As I continue through the presentation and reach the structure I am proposing for them, I explain how the structure provides financial efficiency through a simple operating structure, making sure that both Matt and Wesley are in agreement. I notice that James is not nodding along with Matt and Wesley, so I ask him for his opinion. He raises a specific regulatory issue which apparently neither Matt nor Wesley were aware of, so, thinking on my feet, I explain how the structure could be tweaked to address the issue. James says, "I like it." I move on to the closing we discuss pricing.

Once again, in a sales context, whether a formal sales presentation or a more informal meeting with a prospect, the Meta Pattern is applied as follows:

Associate into the Present or Problem State: gather information about what the client's wants and needs are. These become the issues that must be addressed in your proposal. The benefit you provide your client will be solving these wants and needs.

Dissociate from the Present or Problem States: by talking about yourself and your company, your product or service. Use the prospect's language they used in describing their values, the needs of their industry and business type and so on when describing yourself.

Associate into the Resource State or solution: The easiest way of doing this is to talk about other clients you have helped who had similar issues to the prospect. As you do so, you can switch to using the pronoun 'you' and into present tense languaging. Calibrate to unconscious agreement (nods, etc.).

Then present your specific proposal (but not the price yet – your product does not yet have a value in the prospect's eyes). Describe its benefits in terms of the wants and needs you discovered in step one. Calibrate to further agreement. Now talk about the terms, including the price. Negotiate by offering service or payment alternatives ("We can offer you a 10% discount if you pay in full by the end of month…").

Let's look at an example of how we as coaches may use Meta Pattern within a business context too. After all, coaches are also sales people; we sell our courses or private one-on-one change sessions. If you have been in the coaching business for some time, then you will be familiar with emails, phone calls and in person "meet and greets" where a potential client or student is wanting more information in order to make a final decision as to whether to attend your course or make an appointment, and the Meta Pattern will be invaluable. If you are new to this business, then having the Meta Pattern in mind and creating your own 'business' mindset will put you in a perfect place for selling.

We usually like to speak to our potential clients/students in person either by phone or in real time. This gives us the opportunity to calibrate where they are in the Meta Pattern and helps us to know when and how to move to the next step. We are also keen to ensure that whether they are a private client or a student that we will be a 'good fit' for each other. Here we have already set the win-win negotiation frame in place. Just as in the example above we:

Associate into the Present or Problem State: Gather information from our potential client/student about their wants, needs and values they believe they have about making a change or attending a course. If they are coming for change work we may begin to associate them slightly into their problem. These are the needs, wants and values that we will focus on as the benefits of their change or their outcomes of taking a course with us.

Dissociate from the Present or Problem States: We can then move to explain how our course/sessions can fulfill these wants and needs, or help them to make the personal change they desire. We will use the specific language and 'buzz words' which they themselves have used. We explain who we are, what our school has to offer, what makes us different form other change workers/schools out there.

Associate into the Resource State or solution: Here we might offer a client/student success story (changing names or omitting names to ensure confidentiality). We can also use their values and outcomes to help them step into how they will be when they have made this change or completed the course.

Collapse: Once we see (or hear, if this is done over the phone) that the unconscious mind is in agreement, we are able to move to the 'close' which usually involves the price, any special offers or payment plan options and dates and time of the course/appointment.

Chapter Seventeen:

Using the Meta Pattern for a Formal Presentation

Many people in business have to give formal presentations. These may be to convince your boss to give you a raise, a workshop or seminar to your colleagues to teach them a new skill, a presentation on your company to investors or a potential joint venture partner, or any one of 1000 other reasons. You may have ample time to prepare the presentation, or you may be called upon short notice. You may even be asked to give a presentation instantly, with no preparation.

The beauty about using the Meta Pattern for formal presentations is that the more unusual, more important, and most especially more unexpected the presentation is, the more useful the Meta Pattern is in structuring your thoughts and giving the presentation.

Associating into the Present State:

First of all, take a look around the room. How is your audience? Are they attentive, ready to hear what you have to say? Great!

Or are they distracted; perhaps you got the dreaded slot in the workshop immediately after lunch! If they are in a positive state and ready to listen to what you have to say, all well and good. But if not, you need to change their state. This really has to be the first loop of the Meta Pattern: you need to get them out of their negative state, get them into a positive state, and then complete the Collapse by starting your presentation.

Perhaps you need to tell a joke to lighten things up; this will dissociate them from their negative state, and, if the joke happens to be funny, will take them into a positive state. Perhaps you need to ask everyone to stand up (this movement will tend to dissociate them from any negative state) and stretch to get some oxygen in the lungs (which should begin to produce a more positive state). Whatever you need to do to change their state, do it! There is no point in continuing if they are not ready to listen to you!

Okay, so we have now dealt with the Present State by waking our audience up. We now have to deal with another problem, namely: do they understand why they are there, why they're listening to you? If not, a good proportion of your audience will simply not listen. So the first part of your presentation is going to be about why they should listen; what's in it for them? What problem do they have that you are going to show them how to solve? What will they have at the end of your presentation that they don't have now? There are a number of ways of doing this that are beyond the scope of this chapter, but the same rules of association apply that we have talked about in the rest of the book; switching pronouns to 'you,' switching to the present tense, and so on.

So rather than saying: "I am going to explain our new accounting system to you…" [yawn]…

You might say: "How many of you found yourself not being reimbursed for your expenses for several months? Or even worse, not being reimbursed at all? When you find yourself paying your own expenses, that's a dollar out of your own pocket; or $10, or $100. When you want to take your wife out to dinner, and you can't because money is tight, what will you say to her? That's why you want to listen carefully to what I have to tell you, because when you understand the new system you'll find your expenses reimbursed faster, and you'll be able to take your wife out that great new restaurant!"

You need to stack the reasons they should be listening to you until you see them nodding, until you see that they're in! When there is agreement, then you can move on to the next step.

Dissociating from the Problem:

When you giving a presentation, there is a great way to dissociate the audience. You can simply give them the facts that you need to give them. If you're forced to use a PowerPoint presentation, you will find your audience even more dissociated! When you are deciding what facts to include in your presentation, bear in mind that your audience is unlikely to remember more than a handful of the facts you present when they walk out of the room. This leads to two important rules:

Rule 1: Only give them the facts that they absolutely need to understand the process you will be showing them.

Rule 2: If you want them to remember some specific facts, you will have to repeat them a number of times. And they will only remember a few. This rule is sometimes stated as: tell them what you're going to tell them, tell them, then tell them what you just told them!

Associating into the Resource State:

When you are giving a presentation, the resource should be the positive feelings they have when they are doing what you want them to do. For example, if you're running a training workshop, the Resource State should be the participants practicing the skills you're teaching them with confidence and ease. That is why the skills part of the workshop should be broken down into small enough steps that each step by itself is simple and easy. These steps can then be combined into larger skills.

Even if the presentation is not a skills-based workshop, the same considerations apply. This time the resource should be how they will be feeling when they are doing what you want them to do outside of the workshop. For example, if you are giving a presentation to your boss as to why you should get a pay raise and promotion, you should paint a vivid picture of the benefits she will receive when you're in this new position undertaking these new responsibilities. How much easier will her life be then!

The Collapse:

For this type of presentation, the Collapse is the very next step you want to take at the end of your presentation. Perhaps you want them to sign a contract. Perhaps you want them to call the group about your pay raise. Perhaps you want to go back to their desks and practice using the new expense system. Whatever it is, you need to instruct and to take that step whilst they are in the glow of the Resource State.

Example

You are sitting at your desk working. It's 12.30, and your boss walks by. "Let's go to lunch," she says. As you walk out of the building together, she mentions, "I wanted to talk about this year's pay raises." Now you're on the spot; you haven't prepared at all and you know that once she makes her mind up, that's it. Better think fast!

You take a look at her as you walk along. What sort of mood is she in? You notice she is smiling and engaged, so far so good. You decide to help her mood out a little, and ask her about her favorite topic, her young daughter. She smiles even more, and you're off to a good start. (*Calibrating the Present State*)

Now you have to decide what Present State to associate your boss into. This will depend entirely upon her personality, and the relationship you have. If you have a very open relationship and she values the contribution you make to the company, then you could talk about the job market so that she begins to consider the possibility of losing you. When I was managing teams, I always paid close attention to any of my star performers who might be looking to switch teams! Perhaps you don't feel you can talk about the job market, but know that she values fairness; you could talk about the fact that you didn't get a pay raise last year because of the financial situation of the company, and you hope that the company will be fair this year.

Whatever state you decide is best to lead her into, it's your responsibility to take her there. The more effectively you can do this, the better your chances of getting the pay raise you deserve! (*Associating into the Present State*)

Now is a great time to begin to present your case for a pay raise. What have you contributed to the company this year? Is self-promotion makes you feel uncomfortable, you can camouflage this as gratitude toward the company in general, and your boss in particular: "I'm so grateful that I have the option to work on the Penske File, it was so amazing to be able to save them $10 million..."(*Dissociating from the Present State*)

In this context, you and your potential are the resource! Your boss should be looking at you and feeling that she really needs you, that the company really needs you. Perhaps you could continue your story: "I really admire the way that you were able to build on that premium fee as a result. I was so proud of the way to help the department meet its goals..."(*Associating into the Resource State*)

Once you have shared a number of these stories and you see your boss is looking at you with some admiration, you can complete the Collapse by making your pitch: "What I was thinking of in terms of a pay raise that would be fair to both of us, in light of the contribution I have made this year..." (*The Collapse*)

Conclusion

The Meta Pattern provides a wonderful framework for organizing and delivering a presentation. Whether that presentation is fully developed with PowerPoint presentations and supporting material, or whether it's a presentation that you give on-the-fly, thinking on your feet, the Meta Pattern is a great structure.

Associating into the Problem State

Why does this particular audience want to listen to what you have to say?

Dissociating from the Problem State

Give them the facts and data they need. Remember, don't give them too much or they won't be able to absorb it, and if you want them to take the information away with them in their heads you better repeat it. If you just want them to have the information available, include it in your slide deck, but don't bother talking about it.

Associate to the Resource State

The Resource State is going to be how they feel when they are effortlessly doing what you want them to do after the presentation. They need to either practice the skills there and then, all you need to lead them to strongly imagine practicing the skills afterwards (or both).

The Collapse

Getting them to take that first next step as they feel the glow of the Resource State. Getting Kevin to sign a contract or agree to your pay raise. Getting them to walk out of the door, feeling confident that they can apply these new skills.

Chapter Eighteen:
The Meta Pattern and Sales Copy Writing

If you work in a business environment (including the business of coaching or change work), it is likely that you will have to write sales copy of one type or another. This could be the wording of the formal proposal, information to include on your website, or simply an email to a client. Almost everything we do is designed to persuade someone to do something, even if they're supposed to do it anyway.

For example, have you ever been in the situation where you needed a colleague to provide you with some information, but for whatever reason they're not sending you the information? You can't complete your part of the project; you begin to feel anxious as a result, and the longer you wait for the information the more anxious you become...

Would you like to understand the process of writing emails (or making phone calls) in such a way that they will provide you the information immediately? In fact, they'll feel so good being motivated to provide you with that information that you'll never have a problem with them again in the future.

Sounds too good to be true? Read on! Because when you understand how to use the Meta Pattern to motivate the people around you to do what you want them to do, whether they are customers, your colleagues, or your boss, then you will truly be in charge of your own career. You'll find yourself being better paid, receiving more promotions, and enjoy your work more.

And all you have to do is to become familiar with the Meta Pattern.

Good sales copy will often begin with a problem:
"Have you ever felt anxious about…"
"Are you overweight? Have you tried diets that just don't work?"
"Do you suffer from…"
"Want to make more money…"

You will recognize all these as being the first step of the Meta Pattern. We are beginning to associate the reader into the problem.

We want to point out here that we believe in good karma. If you're not providing a product that provides real value to your customers, you will not be successful in business. The following example uses 'work from home' as its basic idea, only because you've probably seen this sort of thing before. Many, perhaps even most, work from home schemes are a scam and we're not promoting them as a way to make money; this example is tongue-in-cheek. If nothing else, it may allow you to recognize the Meta Pattern when it is being used to manipulate you!

Associate into the Problem State:

Once you've got them hooked into the problem, you may want to sink the hook a little deeper:

"Want to make more money? Can't pay your bills? Creditors knocking on your door?...

Take Eliza: Eliza was working a dead-end job stacking shelves at a local supermarket. She was not making enough to pay her bills; each month she had tough decisions to make, should she pay the heating bill and not eat, or perhaps give her mortgage payment and risk eviction? Eventually she ended up not making payments on her car and her car was repossessed. She was not able to get to work and lost her job…"

Dissociate from the Problem State:

Once more you will want to talk about your company and your product in such a way that is aligned with the problem that your readers is facing:

"Here at Make a Quick Buck we help people like you realize their financial dreams. By providing the opportunity to work from home, on your own schedule, with no skills required, you have the flexibility to earn a second income, or move full-time into this exciting career. Earn anything from $500-$10,000 per week with our amazing system.

Eliza did. Make a Quick Buck provided Eliza with a complete system to earn money from home. Using the MQB system, Eliza was able to generate a six-figure income, paying off all her debts and finally saving for her retirement."

Associating into the Resource State:

Now begin to associate the prospect into the Resource State. In this case the Resource State is how the prospect will be once they have bought your product or service:

"Imagine how your life would be different with a second income. Your bills are paid off [notice we switch to the present tense], and you're able to finally enjoy life, take a vacation, help your family out, get that health insurance you need."

The Collapse:

Before we encourage the customer to take the next step, we first need to deal with any concerns they may have:

"You're probably thinking this is too good to be true, but Eliza's story, and the stories of hundreds of people like her, should empower you and want you to make a fortune using the MQB system. And if you're not completely satisfied, we offer a 100% no questions asked money back guarantee."

And perhaps add a certain urgency:

"This special offer is only available for the next 24 hours, so act now. And best of all, of you have nothing to lose with our 100% no questions asked money back guarantee."

And finally:

"Simply send your check for $Outrageouss-amount-of-money to this address: Shady warehouse, Back of beyond, Nigeria. Remember, you have nothing to lose and everything to gain."

On the other hand, you can use the Meta Pattern ethically and effectively to influence prospective clients or students within your sales copy either in flyers, web pages, blog entries or sales letters.

Here is another example for a hypnosis training, this time from a positive perspective:

Associate into the Problem:

Do you ever have a client session that just doesn't seem to get the desired change?

Have you ever felt that you were lost in your client's problem with them?

Do you ever feel stuck and not sure what to do?

Dissociate from the Problem:

Join us for our upcoming 8-day Hypnotic Mastery Super Duper Course. This one-of-a-kind course exclusively offered by our training center will provide you with the skills, techniques and personal transformation to ensure you become the best change worker you can be. During this course you will explore the core principals that underpin the change process, learn how to make transformations at a deep neurological level, and make generative change for yourself and those you work with.

Associate into the Resource:

Take a moment and imagine working with a client and being:
Totally aware of the structure of their problem AND having a road map for how to help them change.
Able to identify your client's core beliefs and work in alignment with them to ensure deep change.
Performing both overt and covert hypnotic change so that transformation is easy and seamless for your client.
Have supercharged confidence in your own ability to affect change in others.

The Collapse:

Having these skills will transform the coaching experience for both you and your client.

Join us for this transformational course September X–September X 20XX.
This course is open to only 20 students, so please act fast to ensure your place.

Or another example of an even softer, more personal email:

Hi Everyone,

We are so excited that next week you will become certified NLPers. We also realize that we are coming to the end of a wonderful journey with you. Many of you have asked us how you can continue your learning and continue to practice your skills and have expressed your frustrations that you have no one to practice with. (Associate into the Problem State)

Well, we have great news for you. We are holding a 4 day Supervision workshop in June of this year. (Dissociate from the Problem State)

At this workshop, you will have many opportunities to work with clients while receiving real-time coaching from Master trainers. Imagine having the time to do a full piece of change work with a client and at the same time receiving guidance and feedback taking your change work to the next level. (Associate into the Resource State)

We are opening up this opportunity to only 8 students, so let us know ASAP if you are ready to enhance your skills and supercharge your ability to affect change in your clients and in yourself!

It is going to be a fantastic transformational 2 weekends and we know you're ready for the ride. (The Collapse)

Looking forward to hearing from you soon.

Warmly,
Sarah, Shawn and Jess

Chapter Nineteen:

Goal-Setting and The Meta Pattern

Business, as indeed life itself, is about setting and achieving goals. Where you want to be working? What do you want to be doing there? What do you want to achieve by being there? How do you want to feel about it? How does your job or career line up with your values? Who are you as a person when you are working?

A company or organization will also have its own goals. These may be revenue targets, profit targets, expense targets, staff turnover targets, or any one of 1000 different metrics. And within these goals, they will expect you, the employee, to achieve certain things to help them reach these goals. If you're part of the management of the company, you may also be responsible for helping to set and achieve these corporate goals.

Sometimes, your goals as an individual dovetail with the goals of the organization. This is especially likely to be true if you own the company, or if you *are* the company! But sometimes the goals will not be aligned; the employee's personal goals may be radically different from the corporation's goals. If this conflict in goals is not resolved, problems may arise, including dissatisfied and unmotivated employees making less than optimum contributions to the company.

In this chapter we will talk about how to utilize the Meta Pattern to assist in setting individual and corporate goals, and in resolving conflicts between these goals.

Individual Goals

What are your goals? What you want to achieve in your career? Amazingly, many people never ask themselves this question, or if they do, their sights are set merely on the next step of their career ladder; they do not ask themselves if the ladder is leaning against the right wall! We might spend many hours planning our vacation, choosing the paint to put on our walls, or selecting the car we want to drive; work is such a huge part of the typical person's life it is amazing we do not spend more time planning it. I remember going to see a career advisor during my last year of university for maybe one or two hours in total before choosing a career in which I spent the next 20 years! Fortunately it was a career I loved and one that was financially rewarding, but looking back now, I find my lack of planning and goal setting positively scary!

If you don't set career goals for yourself, then someone else will be happy to set them for you; your parents, a career advisor, an employer, a recruiter, a colleague, or even your spouse. Isn't it about time you put a little more thought into this area? As always, the Meta Pattern is here to help!

Associating into the Present State or Problem State:

As always, the first step is to take stock of where you are. Where is your career now? What do you enjoy about your current job? What do you not enjoy about your current job, and

178

wish were different? What is missing from your current job that you would like to have?

In order to fully assess your current situation, you need to associate into it. Imagine you are in your office or cubicle, you're driving your truck or taxicab, you're standing in your warehouse or factory, wherever is appropriate for you. See what you see around you, and hear what you hear around you. As you do so, notice how you're feeling and begin to trace those feelings to the place you're in, the things and people around you, and the activities you're engaging in. This will give you a much more accurate sense of your current situation instead of making an abstract list on a piece of paper.

Many of the clients who come see me to work on their career goals have a single focus: more money! Money is an admirable aim in setting your career goals, but it is not the only one, and should not even be the main one. In planning your career, you should aim to maximize your career satisfaction and happiness, whatever that means to you. Being poor can be a pretty miserable situation to be in, but being wealthy (or at least comfortable) does not guarantee satisfaction or happiness, and having a well-paid job that you hate is a recipe for misery!

At this stage you may find yourself in one of several situations:

- I love my career and am definitely working at the right company!
- I love my career, but I'm not happy with the company am working for.
- I love my career, but there is another career I would love to pursue as well!
- I love the company I'm working for, but I'm not happy with my job.
- I like certain aspects of my job, but there are some aspects I don't like.

- I don't like my job; there's something else I would much rather do.
- I don't like my job, but I have no idea what else to do.

We don't have the time or space to go through each of these possibilities in turn, however, each one points to a certain aspect that could be improved upon. The most important thing to bear in mind is the old saying coined by Confucius, "Wherever you go, there you are," meaning that you should first be absolutely certain any problem or issue is not inside you, and if it is, change it.

So, for example, if you love your career but not the company you work for, you should first ask yourself how you are contributing to your dislike of the company. How can you change in such a way that your experience of the company changes? This may involve, for example, speaking to colleagues about how they treat you, asking for more responsibility, or requesting a staff person which you can delegate mundane or repetitive tasks to. On the other hand, if you love the company you work for but don't like your career, look for internal job openings.

So seek to change what you don't like about your current situation before running away to something that is new, but that may not be any better.

Dissociate from the Problem State:

This is the time to begin to make lists. List what you like and what you don't like. List the things that are missing. List the careers you would like to pursue. List your interests. List your qualifications. List job openings in your field and outside of your field.

As always with the Meta Pattern, we can loop through the steps a number of times, so don't try and get every piece of information just yet. But make a start on exploring the wider world around you.

Associate into the Resource State:

Now as you consider the details of the goal you are going to set, you need to step into the Resource State, but which Resource State should you step into? Here are some guidelines:

If your goal is something very short-term, for example to give a presentation, you can step into a very powerful Resource State such as a state of complete confidence.

If your goal is something more long-term, you could step into the state of being the 'you' that you will be when you have achieved your goal. So, for example, if your goal is to get a promotion to be a manager, you can ask yourself, "How will I be as a person when I have that, when I am a manager?" Not only will this motivate you towards your goal, but you will also begin acting as if you already have it; you will begin acting like a manager. As such, you are more likely to actually get the promotion!

If your goal is more choice between two things, perhaps two jobs, or perhaps staying in one job that offers security, or going for another job which is more risky but potentially more personally rewarding, the Resource State could be how you will be when you have both of those things, when you're finding things personally rewarding as well as secure.

The Collapse:

In any case, once you feel yourself in that Resource State, it is time to begin taking action toward it. Ask yourself, "What is the next smallest step I can take that will lead me closer to that goal?" When you ask yourself this question from within your

Resource State, you are very likely to actually take that step, and move closer to your goal!

Setting Corporate Goals

In many ways, corporate goals are easier to set because corporations do not have feelings that get in the way. Note that the employees who work in the corporation do have feelings, and these feelings may well sabotage the corporate goals unless the individual and corporate goals are aligned. We'll talk about this in the next section.

It is way beyond the scope of this book to discuss how corporations should use the Meta Pattern effectively to set goals. What we *can* do is to show how *not* to do it!

The first step towards setting successful corporate goals is to identify the problem that is to be addressed. This is not always as easy as it sounds! For example, a company may profitably go out of business if its goals are focused on profitability but ignore cash flow. Profit is the net of the revenue less the expenses shown in the company's profit and loss account. But this profit is not necessarily represented by cash coming in the door. Enron is a great example of a company that was profitable on paper, but where these profits were not represented by real, positive cash flow.

A company may even go out of business while seemingly having both profits and strong cash flow. An example of this can be seen in the history of IBM. At one time, IBM dominated the mainframe computer field. They were the 1000-pound gorilla in the industry, and pretty much ignored the birth of the personal computer that held the potential to put them out of business. Fortunately, they saw the trends in time to get into the PC business, where they became highly successful for a period of time. However, once again they missed the true opportunity of getting into the personal computer software market that became dominated by Microsoft. IBM continued to generate profits and cash flow while missing the next trend that could have destroyed the company, the advent of low-cost personal computers pioneered by companies such as Dell. Fortunately for IBM, they were able to reengineer their place in the market once more, as they moved aggressively into the IT consulting field.

Time and time again companies have been bankrupted, or almost bankrupted, simply because they wrongly diagnosed the situation and focused on the wrong problem.

Dissociate from the Problem:

Once a company has chosen the right problem to focus on, they have to dissociate from it in order to solve it. This would appear to be relatively easy as corporations do not have emotions, but in fact it can be surprisingly difficult. It can be difficult because companies will focus on those strengths that have helped them in the past; when there is a fundamental shift in the market, those strengths may become weaknesses.

A great example of this is the demise of Kodak, the photographic film manufacturer. Kodak film was everywhere; anything from a kiss to a sunset was referred to as a "Kodak moment." They made the best film in the markets, and everyone knew it. They missed the trend towards digital photography in the 1990s, even though they were the company that invented digital photography technology. However, they simply didn't want to destroy their own film business by aggressively marketing digital cameras, and as a result lost out to their competitors. The company struggled through the late 90s and first decade of the 21st century, finally going into bankruptcy in 2012.

Associate into the Resource State:

As far as what we said above about failing to dissociate from the problem, a company's biggest resource is its core competence. It is when a company confuses a product or its core competence that it has the problems experienced by Eastman Kodak.

If Eastman Kodak had focused on its core competence – taking moments in time and capturing them for posterity – it could have aggressively entered the digital photography market and perhaps prospered. People are taking more pictures now than ever before and there's a huge market for capturing, storing, manipulating and sharing these. Instead, Kodak focused on its core product and found itself without a market.

A similar story is true at Barnes & Noble. Barnes & Noble's core competence was providing a comfortable and friendly environment in which its customers could browse a huge range of books. Because it focused on its key products (paper books), and key distribution system (retail stores), it arrived way too late into the world of digital book distribution. As a result, barnesandnoble.com and it's Nook reader lag far behind Amazon and its Kindle. Ironically, Amazon itself provides a comfortable and friendly environment in which its customers can browse a huge range of books, the very attributes that allowed Barnes & Noble to destroy its early competition, the neighborhood bookstore.

The Collapse:

In terms of corporate goals, the Collapse is the ability to actually implement the chosen goals.

More corporate initiatives fail at this stage than probably any other. I remember working at a major consulting company. Their core competency was providing highly technical

184

consulting services to their clients, which they did by recruiting, training and retaining the highest quality people.

In order to boost this core competency, the company decided to implement a new employee goal-setting performance system. They brought in a team of highly paid consultants to design a system that would determine the skill sets required by their employees, track their employees' current performance, analyze the gap between the required skills and the actual performance, set goals that would bridge this gap, monitor these goals, and reward people for achieving these goals. Everything would be tracked through a state-of-the-art database that would be available to all employees at all times.

What they had failed to realize was that their employees were enormously busy servicing their clients. The system they implemented was so complex that nobody had the time to learn how it worked, or the energy to actually use it. Shortly after its rollout, the company quietly went back to its previous, much simpler system and everyone breathed a sigh of relief.

Reconciling Corporate and Personal Goals

In this final section on business goal setting, we will talk about the potential clash between personal goals and corporate goals and how these can be reconciled using the principles of the Meta Pattern.

Probably one of the greatest reasons for corporate under-performance is a failure to align the corporation's goals with those of its employees. Equally, the amazing success of companies such as Apple and Google can, at least in part, be ascribed to the fierce dedication and loyalty of the employees who are prepared to work long hours and do whatever else it takes to be a success in the company, all within their business unit.

Having worked in a corporate environment for many years, I've seen both sides of the coin in practice. I have seen properly motivated employees create profitable businesses seemingly out of nothing, and I have seen badly motivated employees destroy a profitable business hour by hour, and day by day. The failure to align corporate and individual goals at best leads to under-performance, and at worst, leads to disaster.

The mistake which I (Shawn) most often see, leading to a failure to align personal and corporate goals, is the failure by supervisors, managers and other management to even discover and understand what the personal goals of their employees are; if you, as a manager, do not know what is truly important to your employees, you can't possibly consider them when setting goals.

In some respects, the easiest way, and in other respects the hardest way, to align corporate and individual goals is to have a very clear, and clearly communicated, set of corporate values. By this I don't mean a mission statement that simply includes a number of platitudes: "Customer service comes first," or "People are our most important asset." Every company has these as goals. I am talking about values that the company actually lives, values that distinguish it from other companies in the market.

For example, I recently visited with a manufacturing company that has been around, and in the ownership of the same family, for well over 100 years. It is truly a family business, and if you join the company, you become part of the family. If I recall correctly, the average employee had been working there for 17 years, and many had been there for their entire working lives. These family values have become instilled into the very fabric of the company, values such as loyalty, taking care of each other, and balance between personal and business life.

Another company I know also has a strong corporate culture, but it is almost the opposite of previous example. This company operates in the financial services field. It is small and prides itself on being nimble, aggressive, and doing whatever is necessary to make money, both for the company or its clients. In this work environment, you are expected to be in the office by no later than seven in the morning, to show absolutely no fear, and to value profit above everything else. If you were to sum up their values in a few words, you might say courage, aggression and hunger.

The benefits that each of these companies has is that they self-select employees. Many people who were looking for a job wouldn't want to work for either of these companies; the first might seem lacking in opportunity (after all, if nobody ever leaves, then promotions are harder to come by); the second company would be an adrenaline-filled roller coaster that would leave most of us exhausted after the first week. But the people that they do attract are going to be attracted by those very cultures.

Then let's assume that you are a manager and are responsible for setting the goals of your subordinates, and that your corporation does not have an extreme culture like the examples above. How then do you reconcile personal and corporate goals? The answer, of course, is by applying the principles of the Meta Pattern!

Associate into the Present State:

What's more, we will see that it's really important to properly identify the problem. The problem for the corporation is that it needs more sales, greater profits, lower expenses, higher client retention, and lower employee turnover, and all of these goals have been set by management. These have been passed down to you, the manager, to turn into employee-specific goals.

Your employee's problems are different. One set of problems they have, and the ones that are most likely to talk about, will include specific benefits they want as employees; these might include the desire for a promotion, a pay raise, a flexible working schedule, and so on. However, as human beings, their needs also include more intangible benefits: certainty about their position in the company, new challenges and the opportunity for growth, feeling part of a team, part of something greater than themselves, and recognition and status. Each individual will value one or other of these more than the rest; they will have a hierarchy of tangible and intangible values, even though most people have never considered what this hierarchy of values actually is.

Your opportunity as a manager who spends time with each of these individuals is to discover exactly what the values are. This is actually pretty easy to do; for example, you can simply ask them, "What's important to you? What did you enjoy about this project? What did you enjoy about that project?" And if you listen to them, if you really pay attention to them without judging or offering advice before you have heard them out, they will tell you what is important.

For example, Susan might say, "Why did Jenny get to go on that course, and not me?" What Susan is saying is that by sending Jenny on the course instead of her, the company has violated one of Susan's values. If you patiently listen, asking clarifying, open questions when necessary, you'll find out which value has been violated:

"I'm sorry, did you want to go on that course?"

"Yes, I really wanted to learn that…" (Susan values personal growth.)

"Yes, you know they won't promote me unless I have been on that course…" (Susan really values that promotion.)

188

"Yes, it's not fair, she always gets to go..." (Susan values fairness.)

The main thing is to listen to your employees over a period of time so you can hear which values are stated repeatedly. These are the key values that drive them. When you know what their values are, you can align their objectives with both the corporate objectives, and also with their own personal values and outcomes.

There is a third problem that also need to be addressed, the same problem we considered when talking about the Visual Squash, namely that the corporate goals and their individual goals are not yet aligned. This leads to the next step of the Meta Pattern, dissociating from the Present State.

Dissociating from the Present State:

I remember being a junior employee going through various rounds of goal setting and objective setting with the manager I reported to. The format of these sessions was always the same: this is what the company expects from you, generate $X in revenue, have Y chargeable hours, and so on. These goals will be entered into the form either on paper or online, and promptly forgotten about. A year later, the next performance review would be scheduled, the prior year's goals taken out and dusted off, and a fictionalized account of my activities over the prior year would be created to demonstrate that I had indeed achieved all the goals set the prior year. For the most part, both the manager and I were perfectly happy to sign off and get the whole process out of the way. It was an exercise in futility that satisfied only the requirements of the HR group that the correct forms be filled out.

Manager: "Hi, Susan, come in and sit down. This year the company has a growth target of 10%. In order to meet this, we're asking everyone to bill 10% more this year, and that's going to be your first goal, okay?"

Susan: "Sure, I guess."

Susan has agreed to the goal on paper, but that doesn't mean she has personally bought into it.

When you, as the manager, align your subordinate's goals with the corporate goals, then the goal-setting process can become useful to everyone concerned. Following step one, you are now in the position where you understand the corporate goals, because they have been given to you, and you understand the personal goals of the employees because you are taking time to listen to them. You can now proceed in a manner similar to that described in the Visual Squash pattern above:

Manager: "I know that personal growth is very important to you [leveraging one of Susan's highest values]. I want you to know it is important to the company as well; they see great potential in you, and they want you to grow into that…"

As manager, you will now wait for Susan's reaction; if you have correctly determined that personal growth is indeed a high value for her, she should begin to 'light up.'

Susan: "Yes, personal growth is important to me, I love to learn and get new skills. The last time the company sent Jenny on a course, not me. It seems all they want me to do is to bring more money in the door."

Manager: "It's true that the company is trying to grow the top line. We are giving most people a growth target of 10%. But honestly, I'm hoping for a lot more from you. I know we sent Jenny on that training; it is important that everyone gets a chance to develop his or her skills. That's why we put together a special training program for you that I think can really get you to the next level. I know this might sound scary, but I really believe you can double your revenue next year, how does that sound?"

Susan: "Wow, I don't know. I'd love to be able to do that. You really think I can?"

In this case, the manager has leveraged Susan's value of personal growth in the goal setting so that a much larger revenue increase becomes a mere 'side effect.' Of course, if you're going to use the individual's goals in this way as a manager, you better make sure that you give Susan enough support over the next year for her to blossom, but if you do, you will have a highly effective and loyal employee.

Note that this approach only works if you actually use the employee's own values. If you had tried the same approach with Jenny (who could care less about personal growth), likely it simply wouldn't work.

Chapter Twenty:

Giving Performance Feedback

Now you have helped your team member to set their goals and align those goals with the company's goals and also with their own values. You now have to give them feedback during the course of the year. How can the Meta Pattern help with that?

It turns out that the Meta Pattern is ideally suited to help you to structure a feedback session. This is because these emotional states you want the other person to go through are exactly the four states outlined in the Meta Pattern. Understanding what these four states are will quickly and easily allow you to avoid the mistakes most reviewers make when delivering performance reviews, and to turn the process into one which will be highly mutually beneficial to both the company and your team member. It will also make your own life much easier.

Associate into the Present State:

For many managers forced into the role of reviewer, a role that many people feel uncomfortable with and unsuited for, the performance review falls into one of two types:

192

A series of positive platitudes that may make the other person feel good about their performance, but which do not help them to grow or develop; or

A mutually uncomfortable bitch fest, victory in which goes to the one who can play the blame game better.

If this is the usual performance review process, then the person being reviewed is likely to enter into the review meeting in one of two states: okay with the process because they know they will receive positive feedback, but slightly bored because it will also be a waste of their time; or, defensive, fearful and angry because they know they will be blamed for other people's shortcomings.

I remember I was recently observing a performance feedback meeting where the manager was going to give negative feedback on the employee's performance on a particular project. The manager was extremely uncomfortable with the thought of giving this feedback, and began nervously tapping their hand on the tabletop. The manager was married and wearing a wedding ring, and throughout the meeting there was the 'tap, tap, tap' of the wedding ring against the tabletop, a sound that put my teeth on edge and probably did nothing to calm the employee. After a brief greeting, the manager immediately launched into a criticism of the employee's performance. Not surprisingly, the employee became defensive and blamed the manager for the problems that had occurred with the project. The meeting quickly descended into a testy blame game, and ended up with the manager writing a negative review for the employee's personnel file, and the employee formally objecting to the review. Nothing positive was achieved by the meeting, a great deal of damage was done to the relationship between the two individuals, and also to the relationship between the employee and the company.

Neither boredom, fear nor anger are optimal states for a useful performance review. The optimal state is in fact one that contains feelings of security, curiosity, and a desire to learn. The employee has to believe they are safe, that their achievements will be recognized, and positive and constructive advice will be given. And they have to value the feedback as a way to help them to grow and develop within the organization.

In order to be successful, the reviewer has to have a positive relationship with the employee. If you as a manager have spent the prior year criticizing the employee so the employee feels nervous or angry every time they see you, there is virtually no chance that they will enter into the review meeting in the necessary state to receive constructive feedback. On the other hand, if you have spent the prior year supporting them, offering appropriate praise, and guiding change when necessary, the employee is likely to enter into the performance review meeting with a sense of trust.

It is of course possible that the employee may simply have a nervous disposition, and even though you have encouraged them over the course of the past year, the formal nature of the performance review meeting may cause them to feel afraid or defensive. As the reviewing manager, you have to get them into the correct state to receive constructive feedback if you want the meeting to be a success. This means that you need to be able to calibrate the state of your employee (calibration has been discussed at length elsewhere in the book), and to be able to lead your employee into a new state if necessary. One of the ways to generate a more positive state is to lead the discussion round to areas which the employee values. You should already be familiar with their values; see the discussion of goal setting above.

You should not move on to the performance evaluation itself until you see that the employee is in the right state to receive feedback. Even when you see the employee is in a positive state, you should begin the performance review by going over any and all positive feedback for the employee. This helps to strengthen the employee's positive state, as well as providing positive reinforcement for attitudes and behaviors that you want to encourage.

Once again, at this point it is important to point out that a performance review meeting is the culmination of interactions you have had with this employee during the course of the year. If you never give positive feedback on an ongoing basis, and you only give a meager "well-done" at the start of the meeting, the employee may well take that message as "Wait for it, here comes the bad news!" In contrast, if you have continuously provided positive feedback to the employee, and to others the employee reports to (in such a way that the employee is aware you are giving this feedback to their superiors), then you have set up a pattern of positive feedback that simply continues into the review meeting.

Dissociate from the Problem:

Now you come to the 'meat' of the feedback you are offering to the employee, areas in which they can improve. This is the part of the performance review where you need to be the most open to feedback, most willing to listen, and most willing to change based on feedback given. The best way to do this is to dissociate from the feedback; after all, the feedback is not about them, it's about some THING they did (or didn't do).

An easy way to do this is to take the object of the feedback, for example, a performance review form filled in by somebody they work for, and put it on the table in front of you both. This means that you should not be sitting across from the person, because you will be redirecting your energy toward them at this sensitive time. Rather, you should be sitting more or less side-by-side with them with the 'issue' in front of both of you. You then direct your discussion toward that object, not at them:

"What could we have done, what could you and I have done, so this project worked out better?"

Associate into the Resource State:

You can now begin to associate them into a more resourceful state. Perhaps you say, "I know you're really good at budgeting, because I have seen you control the budgets on other jobs…"

The Collapse:

"…there was a cost overrun on this project. How could we have budgeted better to control costs or to let the client know earlier what the cost would be?... What I'd like to see is for you to really get your arms around the budget for each of the projects you're working on, really using that strength to keep control of the costs, and communicate any cost overruns to the client at the earliest stage possible…"

You might then loop through steps 3 and 4 for the various pieces of feedback you want to give them. Toward the end of the performance review meeting, you will move on to the final resource and Collapse.

Associate to the Resource State:

First the resource: "Overall, I really want you to know how happy we are with your performance…"

The Collapse:

Then the Collapse: "…and I know from now on you're really going to stay on top of the budgeting, and that's really going to take you a long way toward that promotion…"

Conclusion

Through the pages of this book, from real-world examples and extracts from client sessions, we have introduced you to an amazing pattern of change work. The Meta Pattern is not simply another pattern to add to the change worker's tool kit, another technique or an additional script; it is the underlying structure of *all* change. The foundation upon which all change takes place and the necessary cycle we need to move our clients through in order to affect long lasting change.

At first glance, it may appear it may appear to be too simplistic, too basic, and yet it is from this simple elegance that we can begin to build profound changes in our lives and of those with whom we work.

We have shared how the Meta Pattern is fundamental within change work, how it is the structure beneath the many NLP patterns, its utilization in classical hypnosis, and how it can be applied to self-coaching and self-improvement. We have also shared how this pattern is key within the business context: in negotiations, sales, presentations, and even copy writing.

We hope you have enjoyed taking this journey into discovering the secret behind being a *good* change worker and an *exquisite* change worker. The kind of change worker who can easily move your client through different states, can build vast resources and know where to attach them, how to attach them and why … on a neurological level!

The kind of change worker who can quickly assess where both you and your client are within in the cycle of change and what the precise next step will be.

The kind of change worker who can reflect upon your work and make adjustments and improvements along the way, ensuring that you are always striving to be more and to be better.

The kind of change worker who lives with an open mind and the curiosity to constantly improve.

And now it is your turn to take this knowledge and begin to apply it to your practice, within your private sessions, to your presentations, your sales letters and websites, to yourselves and the many lives you touch.

About the Authors

Originally from the U.K, Shawn and Sarah Carson are the founders and directors of The International Center for Positive Change and Hypnosis is New York City.

Shawn is an international business consultant who has advised companies from start ups to Fortune 500 organizations. He is a certified Brain-Based Leadership trainer, HNLP Trainer and coach, certified hypnosis trainer, Clean Language facilitator, and an award-winning author.

Sarah has an MA in education, having taught for over 20 years. She is a certified Brain-Based Leadership trainer, HNLP Trainer and coach, certified hypnosis trainer, hypnosis for fertility specialist and HypnoBirthing Childbirth Educator.

Shawn and Sarah teach with their partner Jess Marion at the International Center for Positive Change and Hypnosis located at 545 8th Avenue, Suite 930 New York. They offer a wide variety of workshops, seminars and certification trainings in HNLP, Hypnosis as well as seeing private clients for transformational change work.

For more information go to:
www.bestnlpnewyork.com
or
www.changingmindpublishing.com

Other Books From This Publisher

Quit: The Hypnotists Handbook to Running Effective Stop Smoking Sessions
By Jess Marion, Sarah Carson and Shawn Carson
Foreword by Igor Ledochowski

NLP Mastery Series: The Swish
By Shawn Carson and Jess Marion
Foreword by John Overdurf

NLP Mastery Series: The Visual Squash
By Jess Marion and Shawn Carson
Foreword by Melissa Tiers

Keeping The Brain in Mind: Practical Neuroscience for Coaches, Therapists and Hypnosis Practitioners
By Shawn Carson and Melissa Tiers
Foreword by Lincoln C. Bickford MD, PhD

Deep Trance Identification: Unconscious Modeling and Mastery for Hypnosis Practitioners, Coaches, and Everyday People
By Shawn Carson, Jess Marion, with John Overdurf
Forward by Michael Watson